Leckie×Leckie
Scotland's leading educational publishers

National 5
COMPUTING SCIENCE
SUCCESS GUIDE

N5 COMPUTING SCIENCE SUCCESS GUIDE

Ted Hastings • Ray Krachan

© 2018 Leckie & Leckie Ltd

001/27062018

10 9 8 7 6 5 4 3 2 1

ISBN 9780008281847

Published by
Leckie & Leckie Ltd
An imprint of HarperCollins*Publishers*
Westerhill Road, Bishopbriggs, Glasgow, G64 2QT
T: 0844 576 8126 F: 0844 576 8131
leckieandleckie@harpercollins.co.uk
www.leckieandleckie.co.uk

Special thanks to
QBS (layout and illustration); Ink Tank (cover design);
Jill Laidlaw (copy-edit and proofread); Donna Cole (proofread);
Ruth Hall (proofread)

A CIP Catalogue record for this book is available from the British Library.

Acknowledgements
P15 Source: "Wireframe." Baldiri. Creative Commons.
P46, 47, 55, 56 and 57 Copyright © 2001–2013 Python Software Foundation; All Rights Reserved.

All other images are © Shutterstock or © Thinkstock

Contents

Area 4: Web design and development

Course outline and assessment

Syllabus

The National 5 Computing Science course consists of four areas of study and an assignment, which is made up from content from three of these. The four areas of study are:

- Software design and development
- Computer systems
- Web design and development
- Database design and development

This book presents the content of the four areas in a more compact and digestible form than that of a full-blown textbook. However, care has been taken to ensure that all areas have been covered in sufficient depth, to give you a strong position from which to tackle the exam.

Assessment

The grade for the course is determined by the question paper and the assignment task. The question paper has 110 marks, which is 69% of the overall marks for the course assessment (160 marks).

The question paper

The question paper lasts for 2 hours. Pace yourself. Try to find a balance between finishing too early, because you have not written answers with enough depth and explanation, and rushing to finish, because you have written answers with too much depth and explanation. Try to write as neatly as you can, this will keep the marker in a better mood than if he/she has to struggle to read your writing.

Marks are distributed across all four areas of study:

- Software design and development (approximately 40%)
- Computer systems (approximately 10%)
- Database design and development (approximately 25%)
- Web design and development (approximately 25%)

The question paper has two sections. You are required to answer all the questions in both sections.

Section 1 has 25 marks and consists of short-answer, restricted response questions. This section allows you to demonstrate breadth of knowledge from across the four areas of the course.

Section 2 has 85 marks and consists of structured questions consisting of restricted and extended response. This section allows you to demonstrate application of knowledge and understanding when answering appropriately challenging context-based questions from across the four areas of the course.

EXAM TIP

Take your time and read the questions fully. Make sure you understand what the question is asking before you begin your answer.

Assignment

The purpose of the assignment is to assess practical application of knowledge and skills to develop a solution to an appropriately challenging computing science problem. The assignment has 50 marks, which is 31% of the overall marks for the course assessment (160 marks).

The assignment is made up of three distinct tasks. Marks are distributed across three areas as follows:

- Software design and development (25 marks)
- Database design and development (10–15 marks)
- Web design and development (10–15 marks)

Development methodologies

Iterative development

Many software development projects (particularly large ones) use an iterative development process, sometimes referred to as a Waterfall Model. The process consists of several stages that are repeated as required. The stages are usually listed as:

- Analysis
- Design
- Implementation
- Testing
- Documentation
- Evaluation.

EXAM TIP

An iterative development process or Waterfall Model consists of several stages that can be repeated as required.

Stages may be repeated to divide the project into smaller sub-projects, or because problems encountered at a later stage may require the repetition of earlier stages. For example, a problem uncovered at the Implementation stage may lead to the repetition of the Analysis and Design stages.

Quick Test 1

1. What does it mean when we say that the software development process is iterative?
2. What alternative name is often given to the iterative software development process?
3. What is the final stage of the software development process?

Analysis

During the Analysis stage we need to Identify the purpose and functional requirements of a software development problem so that we can design and implement a solution. In simple cases the solution may consist of a single computer program, but in more complex cases it may require a suite of programs, often referred to as a Computer System.

Analysis may be carried out with the aim of converting an existing manual process into a computerised one, for example, replacing a manual Stock Control System with a computerised one. However, it may also be carried out in relation to a completely new product, for example, when developing a new computer game.

The functional requirements (what the software needs to do) are often referred to in terms of Inputs, Processes and Outputs.

Inputs are the data that is transferred from the external environment to the computer program. For a Stock Control System, the inputs might consist of details of inward and outward movements of stock items, such as deliveries and dispatches. For a computer game the inputs could be keypresses or mouse movements.

Processes are the work carried out on the Inputs. For a Stock Control System these could involve carrying out calculations on input data or moving it to computerised files. For a computer game the processing might consist of creating, destroying and moving onscreen objects, in line with the input provided, and keeping track of scores.

Outputs are the data transferred from the system to the external environment. For a Stock Control System these could be files, such as a Stock Master File or documents like a Goods Received Note or a Dispatch Note. For a computer game they could be the new location of objects on a screen, or the scores generated by a user.

> **EXAM TIP**
>
> The main purpose of the Analysis stage is to identify the functional requirements of the software. These are often divided into Inputs, Processes and Outputs.

Quick Test 2

1. What is the main purpose of the Analysis phase in the software development process?
2. What name is often given to a suite of related computer programs?
3. What do we call the data transferred from the external environment to a computer program?
4. What does the term "processes" mean in the context of a computer program?
5. What is the generic name for files, printouts or screen displays produced by a computer program?

Design

Design techniques

A range of design techniques can be used to define and represent solutions to problems. You should be able to describe, identify, and read and understand three techniques: structure diagrams, flowcharts and Pseudocode.

EXAM TIP

Structure diagrams describe the steps needed to solve a problem.

Structure diagrams

Structure diagrams are a graphical method used to describe the steps needed to solve a problem. They are read from the top to bottom and from left to right.

Structure diagrams make use of four principal symbols:

Process	Represents a process or activity, such as a calculation.
Predefined process	Represents the use of a predefined process, such as a subroutine or function.
Loop	Represents the repetition of a group of actions a fixed number of times or until a specified condition is met.
Selection	Represents a choice between alternative pathways, depending on some condition. Also known as a decision.

There can be some variation in the symbols used in different structure diagram techniques.

Consider the following scenario:

We want to write a program to calculate the average height of the pupils in a secondary class. The number of pupils in the class is not known at the start of the program. The program should terminate when a height of zero or less is entered.

The structure diagram for this problem might look like this:

Flowcharts

Flowcharts use standard symbols with text to show the sequence of actions required to solve a problem. Flowchart symbols correspond closely to computational constructs such as assignment, selection and repetition.

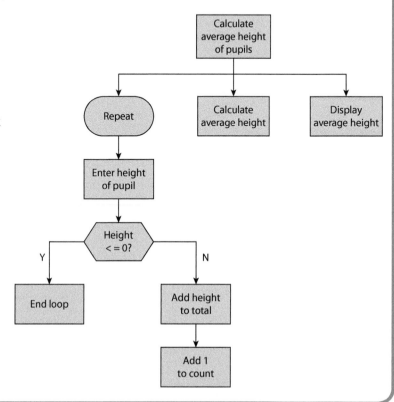

Flow line	Shows the flow of logic between symbols.
Terminal	Shows the Start and End of a problem-solving process.
Initialisation	Shows the declaration and initialisation of variables or data structures.
Input/ output	Shows the input of data or the output of results.
Decision	Shows branching due to conditions being met or not met.
Process	Shows a process, such as a calculation.
Predefined process	Shows the use of a predefined function, often with parameters.
Connector	Shows connections between the parts of a split flowchart. This is often done to keep the flowchart on a single page.

Consider the scenario on page 10. The flowchart for this problem might look like this:

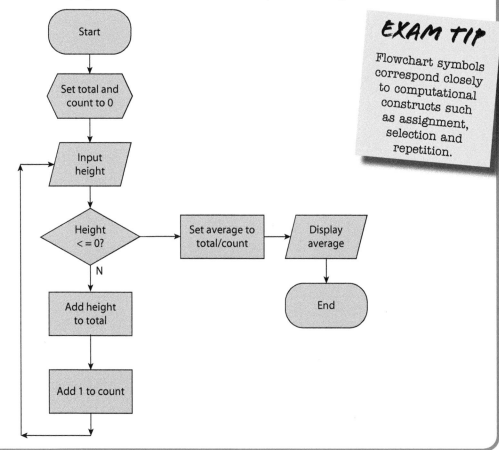

EXAM TIP

Flowchart symbols correspond closely to computational constructs such as assignment, selection and repetition.

Pseudocode

Programs are often designed using a Program Design Language (PDL), sometimes referred to as **Pseudocode** or **Structured English**. The basic principle is that it should lie somewhere between standard English and a programming language. The big advantage in using Pseudocode is that it can easily be translated into any programming language – it is not tied to a specific language.

Pseudocode is used to define and refine algorithms. It is intended for human reading and may omit details like variable declarations or language-specific code. It can look very similar to the code needed to solve a problem, but it does not have the same strict syntax as a programming language.

The design should begin by defining the main steps of an algorithm. Where a step requires further refinement, a numbering system can be used to indicate which line of the algorithm is being refined. Selection and repetition are often highlighted by indentation.

Consider the scenario on page 10. The Pseudocode might look like this:

```
SET Total to 0
SET Count to 0
RECEIVE Height FROM KEYBOARD

WHILE Height > 0 DO
    SET Total to Total + Height
    SET Count to Count + 1
    RECEIVE Height FROM KEYBOARD
END WHILE

SET Average TO Total/Count
SEND Average TO SCREEN
```

EXAM TIP

Pseudocode lies somewhere between normal English and a programming language.

You'll see many more examples of the use of Pseudocode later.

Quick Test 3

1. What is the difference between a Program Design Language (PDL) and a programming language?
2. What does a diamond-shaped symbol indicate in a flowchart?
3. Which symbol represents a predefined process in both flowcharts and structure diagrams?
4. What other name is often given to Structured English?

User-interface design

When designing an information system, whether it is a database or a website, it is of utmost importance that the user interface is designed so that the user will feel comfortable with it. Most systems will use a Graphical User Interface (GUI).

A GUI uses a pointing device (a mouse) and graphical objects (icons) to allow the user to issue instructions to the software. The user interface is the way a user and the system communicate and interact. There are a few elements that you need to take into consideration when designing the user interface.

Visual layout

The visual layout of an information system is how the software looks. The **colours** used in the system, for example, need to be **consistent** and relevant to the subject. The primary goal of any layout is for it to be clearly organised, free from clutter and allow users to locate information.

Readability

In order to be useful any information must be readable. **Readability** means a good design and page layout. All information systems must obey these principles. If the data within a system is not presented in a way that is easily read and visually appealing then the chances of retaining the interest and attention of the user are reduced.

Navigation

The navigation of a system is how the user makes their way around the pages and locates information. **Icons**, **navigation bars** or **menus** are the most common way of allowing a user to navigate. It is important that the navigation is simple to understand for all users. To be effective the navigation of a system or website needs to be consistent throughout and requires minimal clicking to get to where the visitor wants to go.

Consistency

Any system that is designed needs to have a consistent layout. All the pages should use the same **font**, **text size** and **colours**. The same settings should be used for **headings** and **sub-headings**. It looks more professional if there is a consistent approach to the design of a system or website.

EXAM TIP

Look at the BBC website, and note how the look of all the pages is consistent. They have the same fonts, colours, etc. This is a well-designed, professional-looking site.

Interactivity

Sometimes users want to be able to interact with websites and information systems. It is not enough just to read information from them. An example of **interactivity** on a website could be allowing a user to not only look at images of mobile phones for sale, but interact with the image of each phone. The user can move the cursor over the mobile phone and the entire angle of the phone changes and rotates.

Using wireframes

Wireframing is a visual technique for representing the framework of a user interface. Wireframes are used extensively in the design of websites, but they can also be used in the design of any type of software that involves human-computer interaction to indicate how the elements of a screen can be arranged to accomplish a specific purpose. They show the page layout and content, including interface and navigational elements.

> **EXAM TIP**
>
> Wireframes focus on the function of a screen, rather than its appearance.

Wireframes don't normally use typography, colour or graphics, since their main aim is to show functionality. They focus on what a screen does, rather than its appearance. Wireframes are often simply pencil drawings, but there are numerous wireframing programs available, many of them free of charge.

You can find additional information about wireframes in Area 4: Web design and development.

Quick Test 4

1. Which graphical technique is often used to produce the initial design for a user interface?
2. Which type of diagram uses standard symbols with text to show the sequence of actions required to solve a problem?
3. What does a lozenge-shaped symbol represent in a structure diagram?
4. Which design technique expresses the logic of a computer program in an English-like fashion?

Implementation

Programming languages

There are thousands of different programming languages available. They are sometimes referred to as **high-level languages** to distinguish them from **low-level languages**, such as machine code or assembly language. All programming languages share a number of common characteristics but languages can vary greatly depending on their intended purpose.

New languages are developed regularly while older ones drop gradually out of use. Currently popular programming languages include C and its derivatives (C++ and C#), various dialects of Basic (Visual Basic, True Basic, BBC Basic), Java, JavaScript and Python.

Most of the examples in this course are written in Python (Version 3.6). To edit and run Python programs you'll need to use some type of development environment. The most common one is IDLE (Integrated Development and Learning Environment) which is bundled with the default implementation of the language. IDLE features a multi-window text editor with syntax highlighting, auto-completion, smart indenting, a Python shell for running programs, and an integrated debugger which can help locate programming errors.

Data types

Variables

A **variable** is a named location in the computer's memory that can be used to store a value, for example a word or a number.

You may find it useful to think of a variable as a pigeonhole – the location is always the same, but it can store different values at different times. If we want to store someone's surname in the computer's memory we might use a variable called ***Surname***.

It's important to distinguish between the **name** of the variable and the **value** stored in it. The name will always stay the same, but the same variable can be used to store different values.

Some programming languages distinguish between **variables** and **constants**. The value of a variable can change at any time, but the value of a constant always remains the same.

Data types

Variables can be of different types. We'll look at these in more detail later, but for now, the most important ones are:

- **String:** a string of characters, such as a word or a phrase, for example 'McDonald' or 'Well done!'. Strings can contain numbers, for example 'Dave12'.
- **Integer:** a whole number, for example 16 or 1024.
- **Float:** a number with a decimal point, for example, 3.14 or 98.6. These are sometimes referred to as **Real** or **floating point** numbers.
- **Boolean:** variables of this type can only have the value 'True' or 'False'. We'll see later how they are used.

Type ▶	STRING	FLOAT	INTEGER
Value ▶	McDonald	62.5	16
Name ▶	surname	height	age

In many programming languages, for example Pascal and C++, variables need to be defined or declared before they are used. In others, such as Python and most dialects of Basic, variables are created automatically the first time they are used.

Data structures

Items of data can be aggregated into larger groupings known as **data structures**. In this course we will consider only a single simple data structure – the 1-dimensional array. A 1-dimensional array consists of a linear group of data items of the same type. For example, we could use a 7-element array of Real numbers to store the highest temperature recorded each day for a week:

18.6	19.4	18.3	17.9	17.3	18.1	18.8

Quick Test 5

1. What is a 1-dimensional array?
2. Can the data items in a 1-dimensional array be of different types?
3. Which data type is used to represent numbers with a decimal point?
4. Which data type is used to represent a group of alphanumeric characters?

Input and output

Displaying information on the screen

We can display the value contained in a variable by using the **print()** function. For example,

```
print(Age)
```

would display the current value of the variable **Age** on the screen. We'll look at functions in more detail later. The brackets after the function name indicate that the function needs to be given a value to operate on.

```
# assign values to variables

Surname = "McDonald"
Age = 16
Height = 62.5

# print values of variables

print(Surname)
print(Age)
print(Height)
```

The short program shown on the right assigns values to three variables then prints these values on the screen as follows:

McDonald

16

62.5

The lines starting with a hash symbol (#) are comments for the benefit of human readers.

We can use a slightly more elaborate version of the **print() function** to provide the reader with additional information about what we are printing, for example:

```
Age = 16
print("The value of age is: ", Age)
```

would print:

The value of age is: 16

Sometimes it is useful to have a bit more control over the format of integers or float values, for example if we want to lay out data in a table. Python offers a vast range of formatting options – two of the simpler ones are shown below.

We can make an integer fill with 0s to a fixed width by using the format attribute:

```
Count = 4
print('{0:03}'.format(Count)}
```

This will display the value of **Count** as 004.

We can also print float values to a specified number of decimal places, for example:

```
Pi = 3.1415926
print("%.2f" % Pi)
```

This will display the value of **Pi** as 3.14.

EXAM TIP

Remember that Python allows us to format integer or float output in a variety of different ways.

Reading information from the keyboard

Another way of storing information in a variable is to use the **input() function** to read it from the keyboard, sometimes referred to as the console. For example, the following short program would ask the user to enter the value of **Surname**, read it from the keyboard and display it on the screen:

```
Surname = input("Enter your surname: ")
print("Your surname is: ", Surname)
```

Values input from the keyboard are always of the string type. If we want to input a value for any other type of variable we need to convert it to the appropriate type. The **int() function** can be used to convert strings to integers and the **float() function** to convert strings to floating point numbers. For example, we can input an integer or float value as follows:

```
Age = int(input("Enter value for age: "))
Height = float(input("Enter value for height: "))
```

EXAM TIP

Remember that in Python, data typed in from the keyboard is always of type string. If you want to make it into any other type you'll need to convert it.

Quick Test 6

1. What Python function is used to display values on the screen?
2. What does a line starting with the hash symbol (#) mean in a Python program?
3. What other name is sometimes used for the keyboard?
4. What Python function is used to convert input values to integer?
5. What Python function is used to convert input values to float?

Computational constructs

Expressions

In Python an **expression** is a combination of values, variables and operators that can be evaluated to produce a result. The values or variable used in an expression are known as **operands**.

The simplest expressions are those consisting only of values, for example

5 + 9

As you might expect, this evaluates to 14. If we simply type the expression in the Python Shell and press return, the expression will be evaluated and the result displayed on the screen, as shown below.

```
>>> 5 + 9
14
>>>
```

We can also build expressions using variables, for example

```
CostPerItem = 2.49
ItemsBought = 8

TotalCost = CostPerItem * ItemsBought

print("The total cost is: ", TotalCost)
```

If we run this program it will display

The total cost is: 19.92

Arithmetic operators

We refer to the addition sign (+) used in the above expressions as the **addition operator**. Python also makes use of several other **arithmetic operators**. In the following table assume that *a* and *b* are **integer variables** that have already been assigned the values 7 and 3 respectively.

Operator	Symbol	Example	Effect	Result
Addition	+	a + b	Adds the value stored in *a* to the value stored in *b*	10
Subtraction	–	a – b	Subtracts the value stored in *b* from the value stored in *a*	4
Multiplication	*	a * b	Multiplies the value stored in *a* by the value stored in *b*	21
Division	/	a / b	Divides the value stored in *a* by the value stored in *b*	2.3333

| Exponential[1] | ** | a ** b | Raises the value stored in **a** to the power of the value stored in **b** | 343 |

[1]Note: Some programming languages use the caret symbol (^) rather than the double asterisk as an exponential operator.

If either of the operands used in an arithmetic expression is of type float then the result will also be of type float. Note that there is a difference between 2 (an integer value) and 2.0 (a float value).

Complex expressions

Things become a bit more complicated when we have expressions that combine addition or subtraction with multiplication or division. For example, what would you expect the value of Result to be if we write the expression:
`Result = 2 + 3 * 4?`

You might expect the answer to be 20, but you'd be wrong – the correct answer is 14. This is because multiplication and division take priority over addition and subtraction, so we multiply 4 by 3, giving 12, then add 2 to the answer, giving 14. This is referred to as **priority of operators**.

We can change the order of evaluation by using brackets. If we write `Result = (2 + 3) * 4` then addition would be carried out first, followed by multiplication and the answer would be 20.

The rule for evaluating expressions is Brackets Off, Division and Multiplication, Addition and Subtraction (BODMAS).

EXAM TIP

Remember the BODMAS rule when evaluating expressions: Brackets Off, Division and Multiplication, Addition and Subtraction.

Concatenating strings

When writing programs you'll often find that you need to merge or combine two strings. This process is referred to as **concatenation**.

For instance, on the first string might be "Hello" and the second string could be "World". When you concatenate these, they become a single string, "Hello World".

Python, offers several ways to concatenate strings. One of the simplest is to use the "+" operator. The code might look as follows:

```
str1 = "Hello "
str2 = "World"
print (str1 + str2)
```
Executing this code would cause the string "Hello World" to be printed.

Quick Test 7

1. What would be the value of Result in the expression: Result = 23 / 4?
2. What would be the value of Result in the expression: Result = 2 ** 10?
3. What would be the value of Result in the expression: Result = 5 – 3 * 2?
4. What would be the value of Result in the expression: Result = 5 + 4 / 2?
5. What would be the value of Result in the expression: Result = (5 + 3) / 2?

Program control constructs

Any computer program can be written using only three basic control constructs, **sequence**, **selection**, and **iteration** (sometimes referred to as **repetition**).

The simplest construct is **sequence**. We've already seen an example of a program that consists simply of a sequence of instructions:

```
# assign values to variables

Surname = "McDonald"
Age = 16
Height = 62.5

# print values of variables

print(Surname)
print(Age)
print(Height)
```

As you can see, all the instructions in this program are simply executed one after the other. Execution starts at the beginning of the program and continues to the end.

Selection involves making choices. If a particular condition is true, then one set of instructions is executed, if it is untrue a different set of instructions is executed. Sometimes we may have to deal with compound conditions, where several choices have to be made before deciding which set of instructions to execute. We'll look at selection in more detail in the next section.

Iteration involves repeating sets of instructions. A set of instructions may be repeated a fixed number of times (count-controlled iteration) or until a specific condition occurs (condition-controlled iteration). In Python, **for loops** are used for count-controlled iteration and **while loops** for condition-controlled iteration. We'll look at iteration in more detail shortly.

EXAM TIP

Remember that any program can be constructed using only the sequence, selection, and iteration constructs.

Sequence

Let's take a closer look at **sequence**, the simplest of our control constructs. Sequence can be represented graphically as follows:

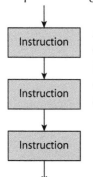

As you can see, a sequence consists of a series of instructions following one after the other. There is no decision-making, looping, or branching. Many simple programs, particularly those that are only designed to carry out a single task each time they are executed, consist of a sequence of instructions.

Imagine we have collected data about the highest temperature reached each day for a week and we want to input these values and calculate the average. We could write a short program as follows:

```
Temp1 = float (input("enter temperature for day 1: "))
Temp2 = float (input("enter temperature for day 2: "))
Temp3 = float (input("enter temperature for day 3: "))
Temp4 = float (input("enter temperature for day 4: "))
Temp5 = float (input("enter temperature for day 5: "))
Temp6 = float (input("enter temperature for day 6: "))
Temp7 = float (input("enter temperature for day 7: "))

# calculate total and average temperatures

TotalTemp = Temp1 + Temp2 + Temp3 + Temp4 + Temp5 + Temp6 + Temp7

AvgTemp = TotalTemp / 7

# display average temperature

print("The average temperature for the week was: ", AvgTemp)
```

```
>>> ================================ RESTART ================
================
>>>
enter temperature for day 1: 18.5
enter temperature for day 2: 16.3
enter temperature for day 3: 17.1
enter temperature for day 4: 19.2
enter temperature for day 5: 16.8
enter temperature for day 6: 18.7
enter temperature for day 7: 19.3
The average temperature for the week was: 17.985714285714284
>>>
```

EXAM TIP

The predefined function **round()** can be used to format output to the required number of decimal places.

The output from the program is shown alongside it. Note that the displayed temperature has lots of digits after the decimal point. If we want to keep this to two digits we can use the predefined function **round()** to format the output as follows:

```
print("The average temperature for the week was:
", round(AvgTemp,2))
```

We'll see shortly how the amount of repetition can be reduced by using the iteration construct.

Quick Test 8

1. Which program control construct uses only a group of instructions executed one after the other?
2. Which program control construct involves repetition of instructions?
3. Which program control construct involves making choices?
4. Which type of loop is used in Python to repeat instructions a fixed number of times?
5. How would you display the contents of a variable named Result, correct to four decimal places?

Selection

We often find situations in programming where we only want to execute certain lines of code if a specified condition is true. We can do this by using an **if statement**.

Think about a machine selling tickets at a railway station. Passengers under the age of 16 are entitled to a discount, so the machine may ask for the passenger's age so that it can determine eligibility for a reduced fare. A simple program and its output are shown below.

```
# check age V1

Age = int(input("Please enter your age: "))

if Age < 16:

    print("You are eligible for a Junior Fare")
    print("Please insert £4")

else:

    print("You will need to pay the Full Fare")
    print("Please insert £8")
```

```
>>> ================================ RESTART ================================
>>>
Please enter your age: 15
You are eligible for a Junior Fare
Please insert £4
>>> ================================ RESTART ================================
>>>
Please enter your age: 18
You will need to pay the Full Fare
Please insert £8
```

Note the use of the **less than symbol (<)** to check if the *Age* entered is < 16. This is an example of a **comparison operator**. We'll examine these more closely in a moment. If the condition is **true**, one group of statements is executed. If it is **false**, another group of statements (following the **else** statement) is executed. The groups of statements are **indented** – this is how statements are grouped together in Python.

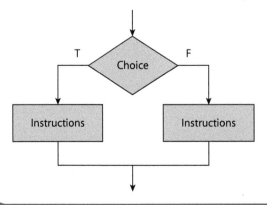

This diagram illustrates the operation of the simple selection process.

What if we want our program to show that users with an age greater than 59 are also entitled to a discount? We can amend it as shown below.

```
# check age V1

Age = int(input("Please enter your age: "))

if Age < 16:

    print("You are eligible for a Junior Fare")
    print("Please insert £4")

elif Age > 59:

    print("You are eligible for a Senior Fare")
    print("Please insert £4")

else:

    print("You will need to pay the Full Fare")
    print("Please insert £8")
```

```
>>> ============================== RESTART ==============================
>>>
Please enter your age: 15
You are eligible for a Junior Fare
Please insert £4
>>> ============================== RESTART ==============================
Please enter your age: 18
You will need to pay the Full Fare
Please insert £8
>>> ============================== RESTART ==============================
>>>
Please enter your age: 62
You are eligible for a Senior Fare
Please insert £4
```

Note that we have added an **elif** clause. This is short for 'else if' and is effectively another **if statement** embedded within our original if statement. The diagram at the top of page 25 shows how this kind of **complex selection** process works.

Many programming languages have special-purpose statements, such as **case** or **switch**, for dealing with multiple conditions. Python does not have a special-purpose statement for doing this. If we need to test multiple conditions we can embed if statements to any depth we like. These are often known as **nested if statements**.

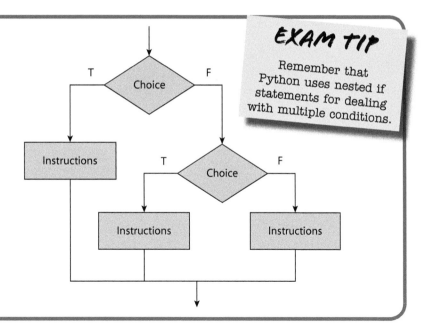

EXAM TIP

Remember that Python uses nested if statements for dealing with multiple conditions.

Comparison operators

We have already seen the **less than (<)** and **greater than (>) symbols** used as comparison operators. A number of other comparison operators can be used in Python. These are shown in the table below.

Operator	Function
<	less than
<=	less than or equal to
>	greater than
>=	greater than or equal to
==	equal to (equality)
!=	not equal to (inequality)

EXAM TIP

Be careful when testing for equality. Remember that you need to use a double equals sign (==) rather than a single one.

Some caution is required when using comparison operators. For example, we might say in English that 'passengers aged over 60 are entitled to a reduced fare' when what we really mean is 'passengers aged 60 or over are entitled to a reduced fare'. In our earlier example we used the statement:

```
if Age > 59
```

to express this. We could equally well write:

```
if Age >= 60
```

However, we could not write:

```
if Age > 60
```

as this would exclude passengers aged exactly 60.

We can also combine comparison operators using **and** and **or**. For example, we could do another version of our rail fares program:

```
# check age V3

Age = int(input("Please enter your age: "))

if (Age < 16) or (Age > 59):

    print("You are eligible for a Reduced Fare")
    print("Please insert £4")

else:

    print("You will need to pay the Full Fare")
    print("Please insert £8")
```

```
>>> ============================= RESTART =============================
>>>
Please enter your age: 15
You are eligible for a Reduced Fare
Please insert £4
>>> ============================= RESTART =============================
>>>
Please enter your age: 25
You will need to pay the Full Fare
Please insert £8
>>> ============================= RESTART =============================
>>>
Please enter your age: 61
You are eligible for a Reduced Fare
Please insert £4
```

Python also provides a **not** operator, which inverts the result of a logical comparison. For example, if the variable *Age* had a value of 59 then the comparison **Age >= 60** would give a result of False, but **not (Age >= 60)** would give a result of True.

Quick Test 9

1. What statement is used in Python for testing conditions?
2. What clause must be added to test for compound conditions?
3. How does Python handle multiple conditions?
4. What are the Python operators for equality and inequality?
5. How can comparison operators be combined in Python?

Iteration

When writing programs we often encounter situations where we have to repeat the same commands a number of times, as in the examples given earlier. The easiest way of dealing with these is to use **loops**. There are two types of loops:

- **Count-controlled loops** are used where the loop has to be executed a fixed number of times.
- **Condition-controlled loops** are used where the loop has to be executed until a particular condition occurs, for example where a specific value is input.

Count-controlled loops

Imagine that we want a program to display the first five entries in the 5 times table.

```
# 5 times table - version 1
tableno = 5
index = 0
print("The ", tableno, "times table")
index = index + 1
print(tableno," times ",  index, " = ", (tableno * index))
index = index + 1
print(tableno," times ",  index, " = ", (tableno * index))
index = index + 1
print(tableno," times ",  index, " = ", (tableno * index))
index = index + 1
print(tableno," times ",  index, " = ", (tableno * index))
index = index + 1
print(tableno," times ",  index, " = ", (tableno * index))
```

```
>>> ===================== RESTART =========================
========================================================
>>>
The  5  times table
5  times  1  =  5
5  times  2  =  10
5  times  3  =  15
5  times  4  =  20
5  times  5  =  25
>>>
```

Again the program runs straight through from beginning to end but, as in the previous example on page 25, there is a lot of repetition of similar statements. We'll see in the next section how the amount of repetition can be reduced by using the iteration construct.

Let's try a different approach to our program for calculating the average temperature during a week. This is a fairly obvious situation for using a count-controlled loop, as we know that the main part of the program needs to be executed seven times, once for each day in the week.

Count-controlled loops in Python are known as **for loops**. The example below shows how we could write our program using a for loop. The output is shown alongside.

```python
# calculate average temperature over a week
# input data
TotalTemp = TotalTemp + Temp
for index in range (1, 8):
    print("Enter temperature for day ", index, ":", end= "")
    Temp = float(input())
    TotalTemp = TotalTemp + Temp
# calculate average temperature
AvgTemp = TotalTemp / 7
# display average temperature
print("The average temperature for the week was: ", AvgTemp)
```

```
Enter temperature for day  1 : 18.5
Enter temperature for day  2 : 16.3
Enter temperature for day  3 : 17.1
Enter temperature for day  4 : 19.2
Enter temperature for day  5 : 16.8
Enter temperature for day  6 : 18.7
Enter temperature for day  7 : 19.3
The average temperature for the week was: 17.985714285714284
```

Let's take a closer look at the loop itself.

```python
for index in range (1, 8):
    print("Enter temperature for day ", index, ":", end= " ")
    Temp = float(input())
TotalTemp = TotalTemp + Temp
```

The integer variable *index* is used as a **loop counter**, which takes each of the values used within the loop in turn. The numbers in brackets (1, 8) specify the initial and final values of the counter. You might be a bit surprised that the final value is 8 rather than 7, but the diagram below should make things clearer.

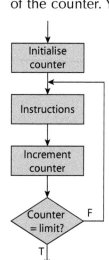

Before the loop begins the counter is set to the initial value. The indented lines show the instructions in the body of the loop. These are executed and then the value of the counter is incremented (increased) by 1. A check is then carried out to see whether the counter has reached its final value. If not, the body of the loop is executed again, otherwise the loop ends. In this example the loop ends when the counter reaches 8, after the body has been executed seven times.

EXAM TIP

A for loop checks whether the terminating value has been exceeded at the end of the loop.

Let's look at another example – our 5 times table program, written using a for loop. The example on the next page shows the program and the output produced.

```
# 5 times table - version 2
tableno = 5
print("The ", tableno, "times table")
for index in range (1, tableno + 1):
    print(tableno," times ",  index, " = ", (tableno * index))
```

```
The  5  times table
5  times  1  =  5
5  times  2  =  10
5  times  3  =  15
5  times  4  =  20
```

This is certainly much clearer and simpler than the original version. Note that we need to specify the range of the loop as (1, 6) to make sure that the termination value is correct.

We can easily extend this program by allowing the user to specify the table to be printed, as shown below:

```
# any times table
tableno = int (input("Which table do you want to print? "))
print("The ", tableno, " times table")
for index in range (1, tableno + 1):
    print(tableno," times ", index, " = ", (tableno * index))
```

```
Which table do you want to print? 17
The  17  times table
17  times  1  =  17
17  times  2  =  34
17  times  3  =  51
17  times  4  =  68
17  times  5  =  85
```

(only the first five lines of output are shown)

Condition-controlled loops

For loops are great when we know exactly how many times we wish to execute the loop, but we often encounter situations where we do not know in advance how often the loop will need to be executed. To deal with this we need to use a different type of loop – a **condition-controlled loop** – which will stop executing when a particular condition is encountered, for example, if a specific value is entered by the user.

GOT IT?

Condition-controlled loops are known in Python as **while loops**. Imagine we want to enter the height of each pupil in a class of unknown size and calculate the average height. The loop should terminate when we enter a zero (0). The program and output might look as shown below:

```
# calculate average height of pupils in a class
Total = 0
Count = 0
Height = float(input("Enter height of first pupil: "))
while Height > 0 :
    Count = Count + 1
    Total = Total + Height
    Height = float(input("Enter height of next pupil; "))
if Count > 0:
    print("Number of pupils = ", Count)
    Average = Total / Count
    print("Average height = ", Average)
```

```
Enter height of first pupil: 62
Enter height of next  pupil: 64
Enter height of next  pupil: 69
Enter height of next  pupil: 68
Enter height of next  pupil: 66
Enter height of next  pupil: 65
Enter height of next  pupil: 67
Enter height of next  pupil: 68
Enter height of next  pupil: 65
Enter height of next  pupil: 66
Enter height of next  pupil: 0
Number of pupils = 10
Average height = 66.0
```

It is always possible to replace a for loop with an equivalent while loop that treats the number of times the loop is to be executed as the terminating condition. However, a while loop cannot generally be replaced by an equivalent for loop. A for loop is the preferred solution if a loop needs to be executed a fixed number of times.

Quick Test 10

1. Which type of Python loop is executed a fixed number of times?
2. Which type of Python loop tests the exit condition at the beginning of the loop?
3. Which type of Python loop tests the exit condition at the end of the loop?
4. If you want the counter for a Python loop to go through the numbers 1 to 10, what initial and final values should be specified?
5. A while loop can always be replaced by an equivalent for loop – true or false?

Predefined functions

A **function** is a piece of code used in a larger program to carry out a specific task. The advantages of using functions include:

* reducing duplication of code
* breaking complex problems down into simpler pieces
* making programs more readable.

There are two basic types of functions; **predefined functions** (also known as built-in functions) and **user-defined functions**. In this course we only consider predefined functions. We have already encountered several predefined functions, including **input()**, **print()**, **int()** and **float()**. Let's review them briefly.

The **input()** function is used to get information from the keyboard and the **print()** function is used to display output on the screen, as seen in the following example program:

```
# input and print functions

Name = input("Please enter your forename: ")

Height = input("Please enter your height in inches: ")

print("Hello ", Name, " - you are ", Height, "inches tall")
```

```
Please enter your forename: Jack
Please enter your height in inches: 68
Hello  Jack  - you are 68 inches tall
```

The result returned by the **input()** function is always of type **string**. This is OK in the example given above, but what if we wanted to do some arithmetic on *Height:* for example convert it to centimetres? We would need to convert the string variable to a float variable before we can carry out the arithmetic. This can be done using the **float()** function, as shown below.

```
# input and print functions V2

Name = input("Please enter your forename: ")

Height = input("Please enter your height in inches: ")

print("Hello ", Name, " - you are ", Height, "inches tall")

print("This is equivalent to", float(Height) * 2.54, "centimetres")
```

```
Please enter your forename: Jack
Please enter your height in inches: 68
Hello  Jack  - you are 68 inches tall
This is equivalent to 172.72 centimetres
```

We can also use the **int()** function to convert a string or float value to an integer.

Predefined mathematical functions

Several common mathematical functions are available as predefined functions in Python. The simplest is **abs**, which returns the absolute value of a number, i.e. the unsigned value. The number returned by abs is of the same type as the number passed to it. For example:

```
print(abs(-4.2))
```

would print 4.2.

The function **min** returns the smallest value in a list of values. For example:

```
print min(5, 7, 2, 3, 9, 6)
```

would print the value 2.

Similarly, the function **max** returns the largest value in a list of values. For example:

```
print max(5, 7, 2, 3, 9, 6)
```

would print the value 9.

> **EXAM TIP**
>
> The **sum()** function is a useful way of adding up a sequence of numbers in Python.

The **round** function rounds a float value to a specified number of digits. You must specify the number to be rounded and the number of decimal places you want to display. For example:

```
print(round(1.2325, 2))
```

would print 1.23

Lastly, the **sum** function adds numbers in a sequence. By using range (which we introduced along with the **for** statement) you can calculate the sum of the first 10 positive integers:

```
print(sum(range(1, 10)))
```

would print the value 55.

Python offers a number of additional mathematical functions, including trig and logarithmic functions, via the **math module**, which can be made available to your programs by inserting the line:

```
import math
```

near the beginning of the program. The math module also provides values for the constants *pi* and *e*.

You should be able to read and explain code that makes use of the above constructs. The sample programs given are a good starting point.

Quick Test 11

1. Which function is used to add a sequence of numbers?
2. What type of data does the input() function return?
3. What module needs to be loaded to use trigonometric functions in Python?
4. Which constants does Python supply values for?

Algorithm specification

An algorithm is a procedure or formula for solving a problem, based on carrying out a sequence of specified actions. In computer science, an algorithm is a small procedure that solves a recurring problem. The word "algorithm" is derived from the name of the Arabic mathematician, Mohammed ibn-Musa al-Khwarizmi (c. 780 – 850). His name is also the source of the word "algebra".

Algorithms are widely used throughout all areas of computing. For example, a search algorithm searches a data structure, such as an array, for elements meeting specified criteria. There are numerous standard algorithms for specific purposes, such as searching, sorting and working out paths across networks.

EXAM TIP

There are many standard algorithms for common programming tasks such as sorting and searching.

In this course we will consider three simple algorithms:

- **input validation:** checking that input is acceptable
- **running total within a loop:** adding up a list of values
- **traversing a 1-dimensional array:** accessing each element of an array from first to last.

Each of these algorithms is shown below, firstly in Pseudocode, then implemented in Python.

Input validation using a while loop

The program asks the user to enter a number between 20 and 30 (inclusive) and checks that the number has been entered correctly:

```
RECEIVE number FROM KEYBOARD
WHILE number < 20 OR number > 30 DO
     SEND "Error, please enter again" TO DISPLAY
     RECEIVE number FROM KEYBOARD
END WHILE
```

This could be implemented in Python as:

```
number = int (input ("Enter a number between 20 and 30: "))
while (number < 20) or (number > 30) :
    print ("Error, please enter again ")
    number = int (input ("Enter a number between 20 and 30: "))
```

Running total within a fixed loop

This program calculates the sum of a known number of values entered individually by the user:

```
DECLARE total INITIALLY 0
FOR loop FROM 1 TO 10 DO
     RECEIVE number FROM KEYBOARD
     SET total TO total + number
END FOR

SEND total TO DISPLAY
```

This could be implemented in Python as:

```
total = 0
for counter in range (1, 11):
    number = int(input("Enter a number: "))
    total = total + number

print ("The total is: ", total)
```

Running total within a conditional loop

This program calculates the sum of an unknown number of values entered individually by the user:

```
DECLARE total INITIALLY 0
REPEAT
    SEND "Enter a number: " TO DISPLAY
    RECEIVE number FROM KEYBOARD
    SET total TO total + number
    SEND "Enter another value (Y/N) " TO DISPLAY
    RECEIVE choice FROM KEYBOARD
LOOP UNTIL choice = "N"
SEND total TO DISPLAY
```

This could be implemented in Python as:

```
total = 0
choice = "Y"
while choice != "N":
    number = int(input('Enter a number: '))
    total = total + number
    choice = str(input("Enter another value? (Y/N): "))
print ("The total is: ", total)
```

(Note: Python does not offer a repeat loop, so we need to use an equivalent while loop.)

Traversing a 1-dimensional array using a fixed loop

This program uses a loop to access each element of an array, to process the data stored in the array. The processing involved is trivial. In a real-world situation it would be more complex.

```
DECLARE scores INITIALLY [ 14,32,25,56,37,67,24,53]
FOR counter FROM 0 TO 7 DO
    IF scores[counter] >= 50 THEN
        SEND "Great Score" & scores[counter] TO DISPLAY
    END IF
END FOR
```

This could be implemented in Python as:

```
scores = [14,32,25,56,37,67,24,53]
for counter in range(0, 8):
    if scores[counter] >= 50:
        print ('Great Score ', scores[counter])
```

Traversing a 1-dimensional array using a fixed 'for each' loop with running total included

This program uses a loop to access each element of an array, to process the data stored in the array.

The processing involved is trivial. In a real-world situation it would be more complex.

```
DECLARE scores INITIALLY [14,32,25,56,37,67,24,53]
DECLARE total INITIALLY 0
DECLARE counter INITIALLY 0
FOR EACH FROM scores DO
    SET total TO total + scores[counter]
    SET counter TO counter + 1
END FOR
SEND total TO DISPLAY
```

This could be implemented in Python as:

```
scores = [14,32,25,56,37,67,24,53]
total = 0
counter = 0

for each in scores:
    total = total + scores[counter]
    counter = counter + 1
print ("The total is: ", total)
```
(Note that "each" is simply an identifier. "each" is not a keyword in Python.)

Quick Test 12

1. Which type of algorithm is used to check that input data is correct?
2. Which type of algorithm is used to find a given value in an array?
3. Which type of algorithm is used to put all the elements of an array into a specified order?
4. Which type of algorithm visits each element of an array in turn?

Testing

Errors

Programming is a complex process and it is easy for errors to occur. It is therefore necessary to **test computer programs thoroughly** to ensure that they work correctly under all circumstances. Errors in programs are often referred to as **bugs**, supposedly because early computers, which made use of electrical relays, suffered problems due to insects (bugs) shorting these relays. The process of testing programs is sometimes referred to as **debugging**.

Three different types of errors are commonly found in programs: syntax errors, run-time errors and logic errors.

Syntax errors

Syntax errors are errors in the structure or grammar of the program. They are fairly easy to find as they are generally detected by the compiler or interpreter when attempting to convert the source program to machine code. The following code fragment has two syntax errors: a quote character ('') has been omitted in line 4 and there is a bracket missing from the end of line 7.

```
1 | # Program 2.4: Syntax Errors
2 |
3 | number1 = float(input("Enter the first number: "))
4 | number2 = float(input("Enter the second number: ))
5 | print("")
6 |
7 | print("number1 plus number2 = ", number1 + number2
8 | print("number1 divided by number2 = ", number1 / number2)
```

If we attempt to run this program we will get an error message and a visual indicator (a red bar) showing where the error occurs. (EOL means 'End of Line'.)

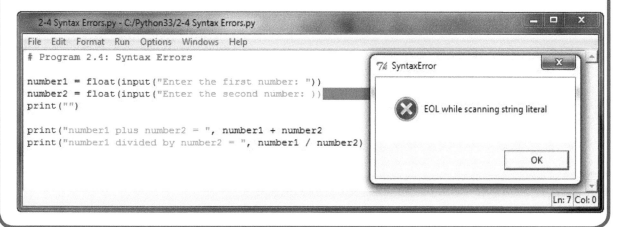

If we correct this and try to run the program again, we will get a further error:

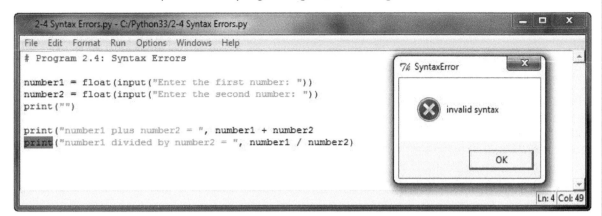

Note that this time the error indicator appears on the line following the error. This is fairly common as the interpreter only realises that an error has occurred when it reaches the start of the next line. The error message is not particularly informative – this is also fairly common. Once we correct this error the program will run successfully.

Run-time errors

Run-time errors occur when something goes wrong during the execution of a seemingly-correct program. One of the most common run-time errors is an attempt to divide by zero. If we run the same program, entering a value of 0 for the second number, the program will run correctly until it attempts to divide by zero and will then fail. The output will be as follows:

```
Enter the first number: 23
Enter the second number: 0

number1 plus number2 =  23.0
Traceback (most recent call last):
  File "c:/Python33/2-4 Syntax Errors.py", line 8, in <module>
    print("number1 divided by number2 = ", number1 / number2)
ZeroDivisionError: float division by zero
```

This can be averted by amending the program code to ensure that division by zero is never attempted:

```
1  # Program 2.5: Avoid Division by Zero
2
3  number1 = float(input("Enter the first number: "))
4  number2 = float(input("Enter the second number: "))
5  print("")
6
7  print("number1 plus number2 = ", number1 + number2)
8  if number2 != 0:
9      print("number1 divided by number2 = ", number1 / number2)
10 else:
11     print("division by zero is not allowed")
```

Any time you use division in a program you should insert a check to ensure that you are not trying to divide by zero.

Logic errors

Logic errors occur when a syntactically-correct program runs successfully but produces an unexpected result. For example, if we have a situation where those aged under 16 or over 64 are admitted to a museum free of charge and we wish to write a program to check eligibility, the programmer might code this as follows:

```
1  #Program 2.6: Logic Error
2
3  age = int(input("Please enter your age: "))
4
5  if ((age < 16) and (age > 64)):
6      print("You are entitled to free admission")
7  else:
8      print("You are not entitled to free admission")
```

When this is run it will always produce the following output, no matter what age is entered:

```
You are not entitled to free admission
```

There is a fault in line 5 of the program. It is impossible for age to be < 16 **and** > 64. If this line is corrected to read: **if ((age< 16) or (age> 64)):** the program will run correctly.

If you need to use compound comparison statements you should always test them carefully to ensure that they function as expected.

Another common type of logic error is the **infinite loop**, a sequence of instructions in a computer program which loops endlessly. This is usually because the loop has no terminating condition or a terminating condition that can never be met.

Area 1: Software design and development

GOT IT?

The following program will never terminate because no attempt is ever made to change the value of x, so it will always remain as 1.

```
x = 1
while(x == 1):
        print("Infinite Loop")
```

The next example is a bit more complex. This program will never terminate because representation of floating point numbers is inexact, so the terminating condition (x = 1) will never be met.

```
x = 0.1
while x != 1:
        print(x)
        x =   x + 0.1
```

Since tests for equality or inequality are prone to failure, it is safer to use greater-than or less-than tests when dealing with floating-point values. For example, instead of checking whether x == 1.1, we could check whether (x <= 1.0) or (x < 1.1). Either of these would be certain to exit eventually.

Quick Test 13

1. What type of error can be caused by a missing bracket?
2. What type of error results from attempting to divide by zero?
3. What type of error occurs as a result of incorrect comparisons?
4. When is a syntax error normally discovered?
5. How do we know that a logic error has occurred?

Finding and fixing errors

The process of running a program with the intention of finding and fixing errors is usually referred to as **testing** and should be carried out systematically, according to a predetermined plan. The programs we have seen to date have functioned as complete, stand-alone programs. In practice, most programs are made up of a series of modules or subprograms, which are written and tested independently and then assembled to produce a complete program. The information given in this section about the testing of programs is equally applicable to the testing of subprograms.

Choosing test data

There are three main categories of test data.

- **Normal data** is the type of data that the program is likely to encounter during a typical run. The program should be able to deal easily with this.
- **Extreme data** is data at the boundaries of the program's capabilities. The program should still be able to cope with this, but it may require more care on the part of the programmer.
- **Exceptional data** is incorrect and should not be processed by the program. However, the program should still be able to detect and reject it in order to avoid incorrect output or program crashes.

EXAM TIP

Avoid the temptation to use 'real-world' data as test data. It does not normally contain enough extreme or exceptional cases to test a program effectively.

Imagine that you are writing a program to calculate the average temperature over 7 days. The program should handle temperatures in the range –20°C to 60°C. The program could look as follows:

```
1  #Program 2.7 Test Data
2
3  total = 0
4
5  for index in range(1, 8):
6
7    print("")
8    temp = int(input("Enter a value between -20 and 60: "))
9
10 while (temp < -20) or (temp > 60):
11   print("")
12   temp = int(input("You must enter a value between -20 and 60. Try again: "))
13
14 total = total + temp
15
16 print("")
17 print("The average temperature was: ", total / 7)
```

- **Normal data** should be spread throughout the range and should cover both positive and negative values, so we might want to choose values of –1, 0 and 20 degrees.
- **Extreme data** should be at the boundaries of the permissible range, so we might want to choose values of –20, –19, 59 and 60 degrees.
- **Exceptional data** should be outside the permissible range. It is a good idea to include values that are well outside the range as well as values just outside it, so we might choose something like –273, –21, 61 and 451.

Our complete set of test data is therefore as follows:

Normal	Extreme	Exceptional
–1, 0, 20	–20, –19, 59, 60	–273, –21, 61, 451

Running the program with this test data will produce the following results:

```
Enter a value between -20 and 60: -1

Enter a value between -20 and 60: 0

Enter a value between -20 and 60: 20

Enter a value between -20 and 60: -273

You must enter a value between -20 and 60. Try again: -21

You must enter a value between -20 and 60. Try again: 61

You must enter a value between -20 and 60. Try again: 451

You must enter a value between -20 and 60. Try again: -20

Enter a value between -20 and 60: -19

Enter a value between -20 and 60: 59

Enter a value between -20 and 60: 60

The average temperature was: 14.142857142857142
```

EXAM TIP

Always test boundary conditions carefully. For example, if you want to check that an integer value is >= 16, make sure that 15 is rejected and 16 and 17 are accepted.

Quick Test 14

1. Which type of test data is outside the normal range expected by the program?
2. Which type of test data is at the boundaries of the range expected by the program?
3. Which type of data should a program be able to detect and reject?
4. Which type of data requires most care on the part of the programmer?

Program documentation

Test documentation

It is good practice to keep a record of what testing has been carried out on a program. Apart from anything else, if the program is subsequently amended the same tests can be re-run to ensure that the results remain the same.

Once the tests have been run we can convert the test plan to a **test table** or **test log** by adding the **actual results** and any **comments**.

Program ID: 2.8		Programmer: A Bunyuck		Date: 1/12/2012
Test No.	Test Data	Expected Result	Actual Result	Comments
1	−1	accepted	accepted	
2	0	accepted	accepted	
3	20	accepted	accepted	
4	−273	rejected	rejected	

Comments could include any problems encountered when running the program and the steps taken to resolve them.

We can evaluate computer programs according to a range of criteria such as fitness for purpose, efficient use of coding constructs, robustness and readability.

EXAM TIP

Testing documentation from previous versions can help us to check that changes to a program haven't introduced any undesirable side effects.

Fitness for purpose

EXAM TIP

Fitness for purpose is about the satisfaction of requirements.

Fitness for purpose (sometimes referred to as **software quality**) measures how well software is designed and how well it conforms to the design. It considers whether the software does what it's supposed to do, from the point of view of an end user. Some aspects of fitness for purpose are highly visible, for example the user interface or the placement of controls, but other aspects like code quality and security are less visible.

Fitness for purpose is about satisfaction of requirements, whether functional or non-functional. In simple terms, functional requirements are about what the software is supposed to do, while non-functional requirements are about how well it does them. Meeting functional requirements alone doesn't necessarily mean that software quality is good.

You have probably come across software that does what it is supposed to do, for example, making online purchases, but it doesn't do it very well. This is often an indication that non-functional requirements, such as usability, efficiency or reliability, are not being met.

Evaluation

Efficient use of coding constructs

Many different computer programs can be written to solve the same problem. It is unlikely that any two programmers will come up with the same solution. Each solution may achieve the same result by using the available coding constructs, but programmers should be trying to achieve the most efficient solution.

There are several areas that should be examined critically to ensure that the most efficient constructs are being used.

Repetition

Repetition can be used to reduce the number of lines of code in a program.

The following program calculates the average of 5 numbers:

```
DECLARE total INITIALLY 0
RECEIVE number FROM KEYBOARD
SET total TO total + number
RECEIVE number FROM KEYBOARD
SET total TO total + number
RECEIVE number FROM KEYBOARD
SET total TO total + number
RECEIVE number FROM KEYBOARD
SET total TO total + number
RECEIVE number FROM KEYBOARD
SET total TO total + number
SET average TO total / 10
```

This program does the same, using more efficient constructs.

```
DECLARE total INITIALLY 0
FOR counter = 1 TO 5 DO
    SEND "Enter a number: " TO DISPLAY
    RECEIVE number FROM KEYBOARD
    SET total TO total + number
END FOR
SET average = total / 5
SEND average TO DISPLAY
```

Note that the first version will get longer and longer, depending on how many numbers we want to calculate the average of. The second version will be the same length irrespective of how many numbers are involved.

The second version can be implemented in Python as follows:

```
total = 0
for counter in range (5):
    number = int(input("Enter a number: "))
    total = total + number
average = total/5
print ("The average is: ", average)
```

1-dimensional arrays

1-dimensional arrays allow the programmer to use the same variable name to store a list of values of the same type. Repetition can be used to store values that may be required later.

This program finds the average of 5 numbers, storing each number that is input.

```
DECLARE total INITIALLY 0

RECEIVE number1 FROM KEYBOARD
RECEIVE number2 FROM KEYBOARD
RECEIVE number3 FROM KEYBOARD
RECEIVE number4 FROM KEYBOARD
RECEIVE number5 FROM KEYBOARD
SET total TO number1 + number2 + number3 + number4 + number5

SET average TO total / 5
SEND average TO display
```

This program does the same, using more efficient constructs and data structures.

```
DECLARE number INITIALLY []
FOR counter FROM 1 TO 10 DO
    RECEIVE number[counter)]
    SET total TO total + number[counter]
END FOR
SET average TO total/10
SEND average TO display
```

Again, the first version will get longer and longer, depending on how many numbers we want the average of. The second version will be the same length irrespective of how many numbers are involved.

The second version can be implemented in Python as follows:

```
number = [0] * 5
total = 0
for counter in range (5):
    number[counter] = int(input("Enter a number: "))
    total = total + number[counter]
average = total/5
print ("The average is: ", average)
```

Selection

There are several ways of choosing from a number of possible alternatives. Some may be more efficient than others, but it is not always obvious which is more efficient.

The following programs decide the grade awarded to a student, depending on the mark received in an exam.

Program 1: This uses four IF constructs, one after another, making use of complex conditional statements.

```
IF mark < 50 THEN
    SET grade TO D
END IF
IF mark>=50 AND mark<=59 THEN
    SET grade TO C
END IF
IF mark>=60 AND mark<=69 THEN
    SET grade TO B
END IF
IF mark>=70 THEN
    SET grade TO A
END IF
```

This program always carries out four comparisons, regardless of the values stored in mark.

Program 2: This uses nested IF constructs with simple conditional statements. Some programming languages may use a CASE, ELIF or ELSEIF statement.

```
IF mark >=70 THEN
    SET grade=A
ELSE
    IF mark >=60 THEN
        SET grade=B
    ELSE
        IF mark >=50 THEN
            SET grade=C
        ELSE
            SET grade=D
        END IF
    END IF
END IF
```

This program may carry out one, two or three comparisons, depending on the value of mark. It is more efficient than the previous program as it does not always need to carry out four comparisons.

Logical operators

Logical operators can be useful when creating complex conditions, rather than using multiple simple conditions.

This program uses two simple conditional statements.

```
IF X > 4 THEN
    IF Y < 6 THEN
        SET quadrant TO 2
    END IF
END IF
```

This program uses one complex conditional statement.

```
IF X > 4 AND Y < 6 THEN
    SET quadrant TO 2
END IF
```

Robustness

Robustness means ensuring that a program will deal correctly with any data input, whether or not the data is correct. Consider the following program:

```
guess = int(input("Enter an integer between 1 and 50: "))
if guess < 1 or guess > 50:
    print("Integer must be between 1 and 50")
else:
    print(guess, "is a valid integer")
```

This works perfectly if the value entered is an integer. However, if something else, such as a character or a real number, is entered, the program will simply crash, so it is not robust. We could make it more robust by accepting the input as a string rather than an integer and rejecting any data that is not composed entirely of digits, using the **isdigit()** function. Any valid data can then be converted to integer and the boundary check carried out.

```
guess = input("Enter an integer between 1 and 50: ")
if guess.isdigit():
    guess = int(guess)
    if guess < 1 or guess > 50:
        print("Integer must be between 1 and 50")
    else:
        print(guess, "is a valid integer")
else:
    print("Input is invalid")
```

Note that the program is now much longer. Ensuring robustness can add significantly to the complexity of a program.

Programmers are often advised to practice **defensive programming**, an approach which assumes that users cannot be trusted to act sensibly and are capable of entering just about any input, whether by accident, or in a deliberate attempt to crash the program.

Readability

Internal documentation

We have already seen how **comments** can be used to add explanatory text to your programs. Python comments start with a hash sign (#) – other programming languages use different conventions. For example, in C comments start with /* and end with */. In Basic comments start with REM, an abbreviated form of REMARK.

Comments can contain any characters and can use as many lines as necessary. They are solely for the benefit of human readers and will be ignored completely by the computer. Internal documentation is very popular amongst programmers as it cannot be lost and is readily available to anyone amending the code.

Comments can help you to remember why you did something in a particular way if you come back to a program some time later. They are also useful to anyone else who has to amend your code at a later stage. You should be aware that in real life programs are often written by large teams of programmers and it is commonplace to see a programmer modifying code originally written by someone else.

If your programs are well written they should be almost self-documenting, so it should not be necessary to add a comment to every line of code. For example, the use of **meaningful variable names** makes programs easier to read. However, it is useful to comment on lines where the code is not obvious or straightforward.

Useful types of comments include:

- **Program identification:** at the start of a program. This should include the program name and/or ID, the programmer's name and the date written.
- **Prefacing:** short explanatory text at the start of each major subsection of the program.
- **Revision history:** details of changes made to the program, including reasons for change, name of programmer and date completed.
- **Tagging:** explicit marking of the end of constructs, such as loops and if statements.

Good practice

- Use revision history comments to show why and when a change was made.
- Make your comments while you are coding – don't leave it until afterwards, otherwise it won't get done.
- Keep your comments short and simple.
- Use comments to 'prevent' or 'allow' lines of code from being executed during debugging, for example printing intermediate values of variables that won't appear in the final output.

Bad practice

- Don't underestimate your audience. Anyone reading your comments is likely to be a programmer and doesn't need every simple thing explained.
- Don't over-comment. Restrict yourself to aspects that require explanation.
- Don't leave 'commented out' debugging code in the final program. If it is no longer required, delete it.

The following example shows a well-commented program. It is over-simplified and over-commented, but it should give you some idea of how comments can be used effectively.

```
1  # Program 2.8: Odd or Even
2
3  # Programmer   : A Bunyuck
4  # Date Written: 12/12/2012
5
6  # This Program reads an integer number between 0 and 999
7  # and decides whether it is odd or even.
8  # Numbers outside the permitted range will be rejected
9
10 # Get an integer number
11
12 number = int(input("Enter an integer number between 0 and 999: "))
13
14 # Check that number entered lies between 0 and 999
15
16 while ((number < 0) or (number > 999)):
17     number = int(input("You must enter an integer number (0 to 999). Try again: "))
18 # End while loop
19
20 # Use mod(%) to decide whether number is odd or even.
21 # If the remainder is 1 the number is odd.
22 # If the remainder is 0 the number is even.
23
24 if (number % 2 == 1):
25     print(number, "is an odd number")
26 else:
27     print(number, "is an even number")
28 # End if
29
30 # End of program
```

Quick Test 15

1. What does the term "fitness for purpose" refer to in software development?
2. What does the term "robustness" mean in software development?
3. Which programming construct should be used to ensure that repeating processes are carried out efficiently?
4. What is the most efficient way for a computer program to store a group of elements of the same type?

Data representation

Binary representation

It is important to remember that although we may work with familiar concepts such as **integers**, **floating-point numbers** and **strings**, everything inside the computer is stored in **binary** format and consists only of 0s and 1s.

Integer representation

Integers (whole numbers) are fairly straightforward. An integer is usually stored as a fixed-length binary number. The range of positive integers that can be represented by X binary digits is 2^x (2 to the power x). This range starts at 0, so the range that can be represented will always be 0 to $2^x - 1$. For example, 16 bits are required to represent unsigned integers in the range 0 to 65,535. The highest value would consist only of 1s, as shown below.

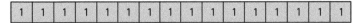

Signed integers can be represented by using one of the bits to represent the sign.

Floating point representation

You may have seen very large or very small numbers written as a number between 1 and 10 multiplied by a power of 10. This is a notation known as **standard form** or **scientific form**. For example: $4.56 \times 10^3 = 4.56 \times 1000 = 4560$ or $6.78 \times 10^{-2} = 6.78 \times 0.01 = 0.0678$

Floating-point numbers (real numbers) are stored in a computer using a similar principle, but instead of using a power of 10 they are stored using a power of 2. The decimal part of the number is known as the **mantissa**, and the power of 2 to which it is raised is known as the **exponent**. A floating-point number is represented by $M \times 2^E$, where the **mantissa (M)** is a binary fraction starting with a 1 and the **exponent (E)** is a binary integer.

The mantissa determines the degree of **accuracy** or **precision** with which numbers can be represented, while the exponent determines the **range of numbers** that can be represented. So, increasing the number of bits assigned to the mantissa will increase the accuracy with which the number can be represented, at the expense of decreasing the range of numbers that can be represented.

This example shows how 6.6 could be represented using 16 bits, 10 bits for the mantissa and 6 bits for the exponent, but in reality at least 32 bits would be used:

Mantissa										Exponent					
0	1	1	0	1	0	0	0	0	0	0	0	0	0	1	1

Quick Test 16

1. What range of unsigned integers can be represented by a 16-bit binary number?
2. Which component of a binary floating point number determines its accuracy or precision?
3. How are signed integers represented in binary?
4. How are characters represented in binary?

Binary numbers

Our normal number system makes use of ten symbols, the digits 0 to 9. This is often referred to as the **denary system**, or **base 10**, because it uses 10 symbols.

As we noted before, computers use only two symbols, the digits 0 and 1. This is known as the **binary system**, or **base 2**. Computers use the presence or absence of electricity to represent the digits 0 and 1. These are known as binary digits, or bits. A group of eight bits is called a byte.

Binary digits are like a light switch. If the switch is in the OFF position the light is off. This represents 0. If the switch is in the ON position, the light is on. This represents 1.

Binary numbers look different from the denary numbers we are used to. Where we would write 13 in denary, a computer would represent this as ON ON OFF ON, or 1101 in binary. We can think of this binary number as being made up of four columns, numbered from right to left:

Column number	3	2	1	0
Value	1	1	0	1

We can use **exponents** to show the significance of the columns by using powers to represent numbers. The exponents are shown by superscripts.

Exponents in denary

10^2 means 10 to the power 2, or 10 multiplied by itself twice. This gives us (10×10) or 100. Similarly, 10^5 is $(10 \times 10 \times 10 \times 10 \times 10)$ or 100000.

How do we use exponents to represent the columns in numbers? From right to left the columns are 1s, 10s, 100s, etc. We have seen that 10^2 is 100. 10^1 is simply 10. 10^0 is 1. (Anything to the power 0 is 1.)

Consider the following example: What is $10^3 \times 10^2$? If we expand this, we get $(10 \times 10 \times 10) \times (10 \times 10)$.

This is simply $(10 \times 10 \times 10 \times 10 \times 10)$ or 10^5, so $10^3 \times 10^2$ is the same as 10^{3+2} or 10^5.

What then is $10^3 \times 10^0$? It is 10^{3+0} or simply 10^3.

What number can multiply 103 by and get 103? The answer is 1, so 10^0 is 1.

The column that is used when we write a number has a specific meaning. From right to left the columns are:

The number of 1s or 10^0

The number of 10s or 10^1

The number of 100s or 10^2

The number of 1000s or 10^3

The first column is the number of digits. The second column represents the number of times we have used up all our 10 digits and so on.

Column number	8	7	6	5	4	3	2	1
Power (base 10)	10^7	10^6	10^5	10^4	10^3	10^2	10^1	10^0
Value	10000000	1000000	100000	10000	1000	100	10	1

Exponents in binary

Binary numbers work in the same way. The first column is the number of digits that have been used. This is the ones column. The second column is the number of times the computer has used all of its two digits. This is the twos column. The third column is the number of times it has filled up the twos column. 2×2 is 4 so this is the fours column, and so on.

The number of 1s or 2^0

The number of 2s or 2^1

The number of 4s or 2^2

The number of 8s or 2^3

The first eight columns are:

EXAM TIP

A table showing the value of the powers of two is a useful tool for dealing with binary numbers.

Column number	8	7	6	5	4	3	2	1
Power (base 2)	2^7	2^6	2^5	2^4	2^3	2^2	2^1	2^0
Value	128	64	32	16	8	4	2	1

Adding up the binary number 11111111 we get:

$(1 \times 128) + (1 \times 64) + (1 \times 32) + (1 \times 16) + (1 \times 8) + (1 \times 4) + (1 \times 2) + (1 \times 2) = 255$.

11111111 is a very long number, but it still only lets us count up to 255. We can use hexadecimal numbers (base 16) as a shorthand method of writing binary numbers, but these are not covered in this course.

Conversions

We need to learn how to convert between the denary or base 10 numbers that we normally use and the binary or base 2 numbers used internally by computers.

Quick Test 17

1. What does the length of the exponent of a binary floating point number determine?
2. What type of notation shows numbers in the form 6.78×10^3?
3. What is 2^8?
4. How would 6.78×10^{-2} be written in decimal form?

Denary to binary

There are several methods available to convert from base 10 to base 2. We'll look at one of the simplest ones, the division method, to convert the number 141_{10} to base 2. Note the use of the subscript 10 (141_{10}) to denote the base used for the number.

The division method uses the **remainder** when successively dividing by two to convert the number. For example:

>   141 divided by 2 is 70 remainder 1
>   70 divided by 2 is 35 remainder 0
>   35 divided by 2 is 17 remainder 1
>   17 divided by 2 is 8 remainder 1
>   8 divided by 2 is 4 remainder 0
>   4 divided by 2 is 2 remainder 0
>   2 divided by 2 is 1 remainder 0
>   1 divided by 2 is 0 remainder 1

We can then write down our binary number simply by taking each remainder reading from the bottom up, so 141_{10} is 10001101_2.

We can check this using the base 2 table shown on the previous page: 10001101_2 is $128 + 8 + 4 + 1 = 141_{10}$.

> **EXAM TIP**
>
> Dividing repeatedly by two and noting the remainder is one of the easiest methods of converting denary numbers to binary.

Binary to denary

Going from base 2 to base 10 is as simple as multiplying the digits. For example the number 110010102 is calculated (using our base 2 table) as

$(1 \times 2^7) + (1 \times 2^6) + (0 \times 2^5) + (0 \times 2^4) + (1 \times 2^3) + (0 \times 2^2) + (1 \times 2^1) + (0 \times 2^0)$

$= 128 + 64 + 0 + 0 + 8 + 0 + 2 + 0$

$= 202_{10}$.

Quick Test 18

1.   What is the denary equivalent of the unsigned binary number 10110011?
2.   What is the denary equivalent of the unsigned binary number 11011010?
3.   What is the unsigned binary equivalent of the denary number 123?
4.   What is the unsigned binary equivalent of the denary number 253?

ASCII Code

Characters, such as letters, digits and symbols, are also stored in binary form. Each character is usually stored in one **byte** (8 bits). The group of characters used by a computer system is known as the **character set**. Each character in the set is assigned a number, which can be converted to binary.

This was originally done using the **American Standard Code for Information Interchange (ASCII),** a 7-bit code that can represent 128 (27) different characters**. Extended ASCII** uses all 8 bits allowing the representation of 256 different characters.

ASCII does not allow the representation of foreign language characters. **Unicode**, which was developed to overcome this limitation, uses 16 bits, allowing the representation of 65 536 different characters. This lets it represent characters in languages like Greek or Arabic, but it requires twice as much storage space as ASCII.

Bitmapped graphics

Bitmapped images, such as those produced by a drawing program, are stored as an array of picture elements (**pixels**). Each pixel has a binary value corresponding to a colour. In the simplest case we could use a single bit to represent each pixel – it could be 0 for black and 1 for white. If we used 8 bits we could represent 256 (2^8) different colours.

The number of bits used to store the colour of each pixel is known as the **bit depth**. The number of pixels in a given area is known as the **resolution**. High resolution images are of better quality, but they occupy more space. They are often compressed to reduce the storage space required and make them quicker to download.

Vector graphics

Vector images, such as those produced by a drawing program, store images as a collection of shapes or objects, such as rectangles, ellipses, lines or polygons. Each object has its own properties, such as co-ordinates, line colour and fill colour. For example, the properties of a rectangle might include x and y coordinates, width, height, line colour, thickness, fill colour and style.

Vector images generally occupy less storage space than bitmapped images. They are resolution-independent, so they can be resized without loss of quality, unlike bitmapped images, which can look blocky or pixelated when enlarged.

> **EXAM TIP**
>
> High resolution graphic images are often compressed to save space.

Quick Test 19

1. How many bits are used by the Extended ASCII coding system?
2. What coding system is used to represent foreign language characters?
3. Which type of graphic image is stored as an array of pixels?
4. Which type of graphic image is stored as a collection of objects?

Computer structure

Computer architecture

All computer systems have the same major components. These components and the relationships between them are shown in the diagram on the right.

- **Central processing unit (CPU)** or processor, which executes programs.
- **Primary storage** or main memory, which holds the programs currently being executed and the data they are processing.
- **Secondary storage** or backing storage, for example hard disks or flash drives, which store programs and data.
- **Input devices**, such as keyboards and mice.
- **Output devices**, such as display screens or printers.

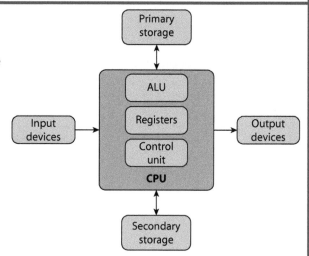

Many of the processors used in tablets and smartphones are designed by a British company, ARM. Modern computing devices often use **multiple-core processors**, allowing several tasks to be carried out simultaneously.

CPU components

A CPU has three major internal components.

- The **arithmetic and logic unit (ALU)** executes the program instructions, carrying out calculations, boolean operations (AND, OR, NOT) and comparisons.
- The **registers** are small areas of very fast memory, used while instructions are being executed. They hold the instructions currently being executed, data being transferred to/from memory and the addresses of the memory locations being accessed by the CPU.
- The **control unit** coordinates the operations of the other components and ensures that everything takes place in the correct sequence. It sends out control signals to move data between registers, read or write memory and control the input and output devices.

EXAM TIP

Remember that the CPU has three main components: the arithmetic and logic unit (ALU), the registers and the control unit.

Processor busses

The processor busses are groups of wires connecting the CPU to the main memory.

- The **data bus** transfers data between the CPU and the memory. Its width, determined by the number of lines used, is an important factor in system performance. Each line can carry 1 bit, so a 32-bit data bus can transfer 32 bits simultaneously.

- The **address bus** specifies the memory addresses being accessed. The width of the address bus determines the number of memory locations the CPU can access. A 32-bit address bus can access up to 2^{32} memory locations.

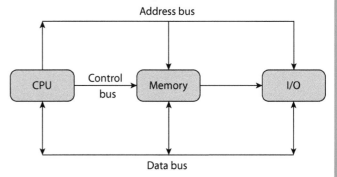

- The **control bus** carries control signals. A read signal tells the memory to put data at the address specified by the address bus on to the data bus. A write signal tells the memory to take the data on the data bus and put it in the location specified by the address bus.

EXAM TIP

The width of busses is important. A wide data bus improves system performance while a wider address bus allows more memory to be addressed.

Interfaces

The CPU is connected to the I/O devices and the backing storage by **interfaces**, responsible for buffering, data format conversion, voltage conversion, protocol conversion and the handling of status signals. Common interfaces include **VGA** (video graphics array) and **HDMI** (high definition multimedia interface), both used for connecting monitors, and **USB** (universal serial bus), used for connecting a range of devices, including mice, printers and webcams.

Quick Test 20

1. What is the name given to the groups of wires connecting the CPU to the main memory?
2. Which group of wires is responsible for starting read and write operations?
3. What is an HDMI interface used for?
4. Which type of interface is a printer normally connected to?

Interpreters and compilers

Although it is much easier for humans to write computer programs in a high-level language such as Python or Java, computers can only deal with programs written in their native language: **machine code**, also called binary code or object code.

Each type of processor has its own specific machine code. Most PCs use Intel or AMD (Advanced Micro Devices) processors. These are very similar and execute the same machine code. However, most mobile devices use ARM (Advanced Research Machines) processors, which run a completely different type of machine code.

The Intel/AMD processors belong to a category known as **complex instruction set computers (CISC)**. They have hundreds of complex machine code instructions, so a single instruction can handle almost any requirement that may occur. ARM processors belong to a category known as **reduced instruction set computers (RISC)**. They have a relatively small number of simple machine code instructions, which can execute very rapidly. When complex instructions are required they are created by combining simpler instructions.

All high-level language programs must be translated into machine code before they can be executed. There are two different approaches to translation. **Compilers** translate a complete program into a standalone machine code program that can then be executed, while **interpreters** translate a program line-by-line and execute each line as soon as it is translated. Both approaches have their advantages and disadvantages – we will look at these in more detail shortly.

People sometimes try to classify programming languages as compiled or interpreted, but in practice most programming languages can be translated by either method. However, languages are often written with a particular implementation in mind, so some languages may be biased towards a particular type of translation, for example C was designed to be compiled whereas Java was designed to be interpreted. However, that does not mean that Java compilers or C interpreters do not exist.

EXAM TIP

Compilers and interpreters are processor-specific. A compiler and/or an interpreter must be written for each type of processor that a program is expected to run on.

Compilers

As we have already noted, a compiler takes a complete program as input and translates it into an equivalent machine code program. This process is known as compilation and can be broken down into four stages: lexical analysis, syntactical analysis, code generation and optimisation.

In the **lexical analysis** stage the compiler analyses the source code, input as a stream of characters, and tries to recognise entities that are meaningful in terms of the programming language. For example, the input

`avg = (num1 + num2) / 2`

might be recognised as consisting of:

<variable>

<assignment operator>

<open bracket>

<variable>

<addition operator>

<variable>

<close bracket>

<division operator>

<number>

During the **syntactical analysis** stage the compiler attempts to turn the recognised entities into instructions that are meaningful in terms of the grammar of the programming language. For example, it might decide that the example given above means: 'add the second variable to the third variable and divide the sum by two, placing the result in the first variable'.

During the **code generation** phase, the compiler attempts to produce a machine code program that will carry out the required instructions.

Once these steps have been carried out for each line of the program, a complete machine code program can be produced. Once this has been done the compiler enters the **optimisation** phase, where it tries to ensure that the generated code is as efficient as possible.

Quick Test 21

1. Which type of processor has a small number of machine code instructions that can be executed very rapidly?

2. During which stage of the compilation process does the compiler analyse the source code and try to recognise entities that are meaningful in terms of the programming language?

3. Programming languages can be classified as compiled or interpreted. True or false?

4. What is the final stage of the compilation process?

Interpreters

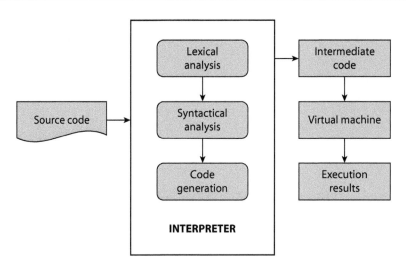

An interpreter operates on a line-by-line basis, going through the lexical analysis, syntactical analysis and code generation phases in a similar manner to a compiler, but in this case, rather than generating machine code for a real machine, the code generation phase produces an **intermediate code**, sometimes referred to as **Bytecode**. This intermediate code is the machine code for an **abstract** or **virtual machine**, i.e. a computer program that emulates the operation of a real computer.

The code is then executed on the virtual machine and the interpreter moves on to process the next line. Note that, unlike a compiler, an interpreter cannot carry out optimisation as it never has access to the whole program – each line is executed as soon as it has been translated.

EXAM TIP

Interpreted code is executed on a virtual machine.

Advantages and disadvantages

Both compilers and interpreters have their own advantages and disadvantages – some of these are listed in the tables below.

COMPILERS	
Advantages	**Disadvantages**
All errors can be found in a single pass. Generated code is highly optimised and runs efficiently. Once the program has been compiled it can be executed many times without recompiling.	Errors can't be found until a program is complete and ready for compilation. Compilation of large programs can take a long time. If anything is changed, the whole program needs to be recompiled.

INTERPRETERS	
Advantages	**Disadvantages**
Errors can be located during program development. Programs can be run again as soon as they are amended – no need to recompile.	Programs generally stop after the first error is encountered, so it may take several runs to find them all. Execution time is slow in comparison to compiled code. Programs cannot be optimised.

EXAM TIP

The best of all possible worlds is to have both a compiler and an interpreter available for the same language. The interpreter can be used during program development and then, once the program is completed and debugged, it can be compiled to produce a fast and efficient version for regular use.

Quick Test 22

1. Why can't interpreters carry out optimisation in the same way as compilers?
2. What type of code is generated by an interpreter?
3. What is a virtual machine?
4. Why are interpreters preferred over compilers for program development?

Environmental impact

The energy a computer system consumes when it is in use contributes significantly to the environmental footprint of the manufacturer. It also contributes significantly to your own environmental footprint.

With climate change at the forefront of people's minds, companies must ensure that they are seen to be green, and environmentally friendly. There are several ways in which a company, organisation or individual user can reduce the amount of energy they use, including monitor settings, power-down settings and leaving computers on standby.

The amount of power consumed by a computer system depends on the individual system and its hardware components. High-end computer systems consume more power than an office computer system that uses low-end hardware. Huge companies like Amazon and Google run thousands of computer systems and servers and must have strategies in place to help them minimise power consumption.

Many computer systems have built-in energy-saving features, such as ambient light sensors that automatically reduce the brightness of a monitor, to systems that automatically go into standby mode or power down after a given delay. Individual users can configure their computers to save energy by using built-in power-saving features, turning off the monitor instead of using a screensaver and disabling services that are not currently needed, such as WiFi.

EXAM TIP

Effective power management can lessen the environmental impact of computers.

Security precautions

Firewalls

A firewall is a program or hardware device that filters the data coming through the Internet connection into your private network or computer system. If an incoming piece of data does not match set criteria, then it does not get through the filters.

Encryption

Encryption is a method of security where confidential data is encoded so that even if it is hacked into, the data is not of any use to the hackers. The data can only be decoded by a software key to turn it back into its original state. Encrypted hard drives and USB flash drives are becoming more common. Emails are often encrypted using a system called PGP (Pretty Good Privacy).

Quick Test 23

1. What technology is used to adjust the brightness of a monitor to suit current conditions?
2. Why should services such as WiFi be turned off when they are not currently needed?
3. What security technique prevents unauthorised access to your computer via a network?
4. What term describes the encoding of data so that it is meaningless to unauthorised users?

Analysis

A **database** is an organised collection of information that can easily be accessed, managed and updated. The data is organised into rows, columns and tables, indexed to allow easy access. Data can be added, deleted or amended. Queries can be run against the database to extract information.

A simple database, sometimes referred to as a **flat file database**, can consist of a single file or table, but most databases consist of multiple tables, linked by means of keys. These are known as **relational databases**, as the keys define relationships between the tables.

Relational databases generally undergo a process known as **normalisation**, designed to create the most efficient collection of tables. Normalisation is a fairly complex process and is outwith the scope of this course. In the following examples we will restrict ourselves to simple databases consisting of only two tables.

Initially we'll look at **Ionian Apartments**, a travel agent that uses a database to store details of holiday apartments available on the Ionian Islands (Corfu, Ithaca, Kefalonia and Zante).

The first step in designing a database is to determine its **functional requirements**. These specify what the database must be able to do. They can be derived from the questions likely to be asked by the end-users (potential customers or travel agency staff). For example:

- Can I fly to Ithaca?
- Is there a ferry to Kefalonia?
- Does Mikos Apartments, Corfu, offer a shuttle to the airport?
- Are there any apartments on Zante that offer family rooms?
- Which apartments in Lixouri, Kefalonia, have a pool?
- Which apartments on Corfu offer the earliest check-in?

This list is only illustrative – there are many more possible questions. As we will see shortly, all of these queries, and many others, can be resolved using a simple database with only two tables.

EXAM TIP

Functional requirements are often determined by questioning the prospective users of a database.

Quick Test 24

1. Which kind of database consists of only a single file or table?
2. Which kind of database is made up of multiple tables, linked by keys?
3. What are the three principal operations that can be carried out on a database?
4. What is the main purpose of the analysis stage in database design?

Design

Entity-Relationship Diagrams

An **Entity-Relationship Diagram** (ERD) is a graphical representation of the entities in a system. It is used to illustrate the relationship that exists between two or more entities. Entities are related to each other mainly by **shared keys** (primary keys, also known as main keys, and foreign keys). This allows us to navigate through the database and process queries. It is useful to show these relationships in a diagram known as an **Entity Model**. The diagram has two symbols:

A box represents each entity and a connector represents each relationship.

The connection shown above is called a **one-to-many relationship**, the left end being the one and the right the many. The diagram is constructed by linking entities that are related by means of their keys. An ERD is usually constructed in a top-down left-to-right manner so that it reads naturally, like a page of text, or a screen. We would normally begin with any entity that has foreign keys and link it to its partner. In our example this means that we would begin with Island and Apartment and link them as shown in the diagram above.

This tells us two things: first, it indicates that "one Island <has some relationship to> many Apartments". We could also express this as "An Island has many Apartments". The second thing this diagram tells us is that the Apartment entity contains the key of Island, since the "many" symbol is attached to the Apartment entity. This is an important concept which you should always remember when constructing ERDs.

The ERDs shown in the following examples use **crow's feet notation** to describe relationships between entities, but alternative notations can also be used.

As noted earlier, Ionian Apartments uses a database to store the details of holiday apartments available on various Greek islands. The island and apartment details are stored as two entities, Island and Apartment.

The following diagram shows the entities and their attributes. The primary key uniquely identifies any row in a table. Only one row can have a given primary key. Primary keys are underlined. **Foreign keys** create links between tables. Foreign keys are marked with an asterisk.

Entity: Island
islandID
islandName
islandAirport
islandFerry

Entity: Apartment
aptID
islandID*
aptName
aptTown
aptPool
aptType
aptShuttle
aptRating
aptCheckin

EXAM TIP

Entity-relationship models show whether the relationship between entities is one-to-one, one-to-many or many-to-one.

Quick Test 25

1. What purpose do keys serve in a database?
2. Which two types of keys are used?
3. What type of relationship exists when one row in a table can be linked with many rows in another table?
4. Which notation is often used to describe relationships between entities?

Data dictionary

The data dictionary provides additional information about the attributes of each table. The following diagram shows the data dictionary for the scenario described previously.

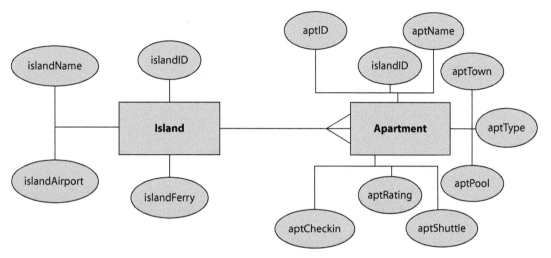

The data dictionary provides the following information for each entity:

*   entity name
*   primary and foreign keys.

It includes the following information for each attribute:

*   attribute name
*   attribute type:
    *   text (alphanumeric and/or special characters)
    *   number (integer or real)
    *   date (e.g. 19/03/2020)
    *   time (e.g. 14:30)
    *   Boolean (Yes/No)
*   attribute size (length (text) or precision (numeric))
*   validation:
    *   presence check (must be present?)
    *   restricted choice (Male/Female)
    *   field length (maximum number of characters)
    *   range (e.g. year 2018–2020).

EXAM TIP

A data dictionary provides additional information about entities and their attributes.

This information is summarised in the following table.

Attribute	Type	Comments	Sample values
aptID	text	Primary key	KEF23
islandID*	text	Foreign key. ID of island.	ISL001
aptName	text	Name of apartment	Minerva Apartments, Petros Studios etc.
aptTown	text	Location of apartment	Poros, Lixouri, Argostoli etc.
aptPool	Boolean	Is there a pool?	Yes / No
aptType	text	Type of apartment	Studio, Double, Twin, Family
aptShuttle	Boolean	Shuttle to airport or ferry terminal?	Yes / No
apt Rating	numeric	1 to 5 stars	e.g. 3
aptCheckin	time	Earliest Check-In time	e.g. 14:00

Quick Test 26

1. What is the function of a data dictionary?
2. What information does a data dictionary provide for each entity?
3. What information does a data dictionary provide for each attribute?
4. What do we call checks made on the characteristics of an attribute, such as range or length?

Designing a solution

The main language used for extracting information from databases is **Structured Query Language (SQL)**. It exists in several forms, e.g. Oracle SQL, IBM SQL, MySQL, Microsoft Access SQL. These all consist of a common core, but may have different features added by the vendor. The solutions given below have been tested using Microsoft Access SQL, but it is unlikely that significant changes would be required to use another version.

The solution to any query is likely to involve:

- one or more tables
- fields
- search criteria
- sort order (where relevant).

You should always plan the design of a query prior to producing the required SQL code.

Think carefully about the fields that are required – this will help you to identify the table or tables needed and will also allow you to consider the purpose of the query (search and/or sort), together with any required search criteria and/or sort order. Planning will help you to reduce the number of errors encountered when working with SQL code.

A simple table template, like as the one given below, can be used to plan the design of an SQL query.

Field(s)	
Table(s)	
Search criteria	
Sort order	

Example 1

Design a query to list the names of all islands that have an airport.

Field(s)	islandName
Table(s)	Island
Search criteria	islandAirport = true
Sort order	

Example 2

Design a query to list the island name, apartment town, apartment name and star rating, for all apartments with a swimming pool and a rating of at least 3 stars.

Field(s)	islandName, aptTown, aptName, aptRating
Table(s)	Island, Apartment
Search Criteria	aptPool = true, aptRating >= 3
Sort Order	

Example 3

Design a query to list the apartment name, town and airport details of any apartment on Zante.

Field(s)	islandID, aptName, aptTown, islandAirport
Table(s)	Island, Apartment
Search Criteria	islandName = Zante, islandAirport=true
Sort Order	

Example 4

Design a query to list the island name, town name and apartment name of all apartments that have a swimming pool. These details should be listed in alphabetical order of island name.

Field(s)	islandName, aptTown, aptName, aptPool
Table(s)	Island, Apartment
Search Criteria	aptPool = true
Sort Order	Alphabetical order of island name

Example 5

Design a query to list the apartment name, island, town and check-in time, of all apartments that allow check in before 15:00. These details should be displayed so that the hotel with the highest rating is listed first.

Field(s)	aptName, islandName, aptTown, aptCheckin
Table(s)	Island, Apartment
Search Criteria	AptCheckin < 15:00 = true
Sort Order	Descending order of rating

Referential integrity

Referential integrity is a feature of relational database management systems that ensures that the relationships between tables in a database remain accurate by preventing the entry of inaccurate data or linking to data that doesn't exist. It is used to manage the relationships between primary and foreign keys.

For example, when adding a new apartment to the database described above, the island on which it is located needs to be specified. IslandID is the foreign key in the Apartment table and the primary key in the Island table.

To preserve the integrity of the data a set of rules needs to be observed.

- Insertion of an apartment in the Apartment table should only be permitted if their islandID already exists in the Island table.

- Deletion of an island in the Island table should only be permitted if there are no apartments located on that island.

- Changing the value of an islandID in the island table should only be permitted if there are no apartments located on that island.

- Changing the value of an islandID in the apartment table should only be permitted if the new value exists in the island table.

If any of the above can happen then we have data in an inconsistent state. The integrity of the data is compromised.

Relational database management systems, like Access, Oracle or MySQL, allow enforcement of referential integrity rules. If a user tries to break any of the rules, an error message will be displayed and the change will not take place.

Implementation

We now can implement our database. Using **Microsoft Access** we can create tables in the **Design View**, as follows.

Start by creating the table structure by clicking Table Design on the Create tab, in the Tables group. The graphic below shows the creation of the Apartment table.

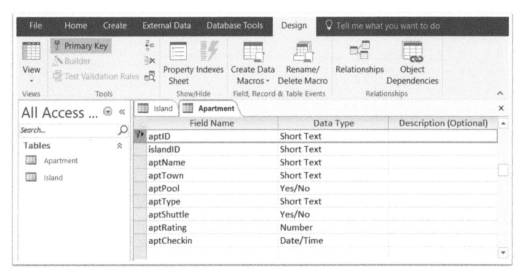

For each field in your table, type a name in the **Field Name** column, and then choose a data type from the **Data Type** list. You can also type a description for each field in the **Description** column.

Now click **Save** on the **File** tab.

We can now create a relationship between our tables by clicking **Relationships** on the **Database Tools** tab, in the **Relationships** group. The **Show Table** dialog box should appear automatically. If it doesn't appear, click **Show Table**, on the **Design tab**, in the **Relationships** group.

Choose one or more tables, then click **Add**. when you have finished adding tables, click **Close**. Drag a field (normally the primary key) from one table to the same field (the foreign key) in the other table.

EXAM TIP

In Microsoft Access, database tables are created in Design View and populated in Datasheet view.

The **Edit Relationships** dialog box will appear. Check that the field names shown are the common fields for the relationship. You can enforce referential integrity for this relationship by selecting the **Enforce Referential Integrity** box.

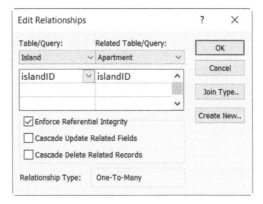

Click **Create**. The Relationship should now be shown as follows:

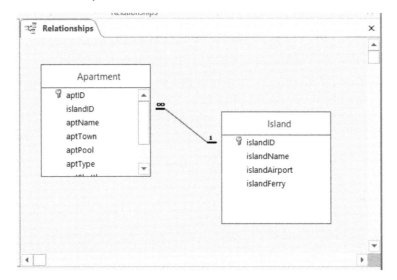

Click Save to save your changes.

You can then switch to **Datasheet** view to enter data, or use some other method, such as pasting, or importing.

Quick Test 27

1. Which four elements are normally involved in the design of a query?
2. What is the purpose of referential integrity?
3. What are the three main steps involved in creating a database?
4. How are relationships created?

SQL operations

We are going to look at some useful SQL operations for pre-populated relational databases, with a maximum of two linked tables. One of the most useful SQL commands is the SELECT statement, which can be used to choose records meeting specified criteria from a database.

The overall format of the statement is as follows:

> SELECT *fields*
>
> FROM *tables*
>
> WHERE *conditions*

We can specify **complex conditions** using the relational operators: AND, OR, <, >, = . Output can be sorted in ascending or descending order on a maximum of two fields.

As we have already noted, Structured Query Language (SQL) is a special purpose programming language which is widely used for storing, manipulating and retrieving data in relational databases. Although most database systems use SQL, there are some differences between different dialects or versions. However, standard SQL commands such as SELECT, INSERT, UPDATE and DELETE are common to them all.

We will use the following relational database to exemplify the SQL commands: The Central Scotland Darts League uses a relational database to store details of teams and players in two separate tables called Team and Player. The structure of these tables is shown below.

Player	Team
playerID	teamID
playerForename	teamName
playerSurname	teamDistrict
playerDOB	teamTown
playerAge	teamVenue
playerPoints	teamContact
teamID*	teamEmail
	teamPhone

Quick Test 28

1. What is the general format of an SQL SELECT statement?
2. How do we specify complex conditions in SQL?
3. How many fields can an SQL query be sorted on?

Sample records for each table could be as follows:

Player	Team
PLAY1234	TEAM005
Barry	Govan Gophers
Soap	West
10/12/1978	Glasgow
30	Govan FC
9534	Robin Banks
TEAM005	rbanks@gmail.com
	0141 622 2323

The following examples make use of Microsoft Access SQL. Slight changes may be required with other dialects of SQL.

Searching a database

The SELECT statement is used to specify the fields to be displayed. It is followed by the field names, separated by commas.

The FROM clause gives the names of the database table(s) required by the query.

The WHERE clause specifies the criteria to be met. It is followed by the field name, a relational operator ($<$, $>$, $=$) and the information required. Text must be placed inside inverted commas.

```
SELECT fieldName1, fieldName2, fieldName3, etc
FROM tableName
WHERE fieldName = data;
```

Example 1: Display the team name, town, contact person and e-mail address for all teams in the East district:

```
SELECT teamName, teamTown, teamContact, teamEmail
FROM Team
WHERE teamDistrict = "East";
```

Complex queries

The logical operators (AND, OR) can be used to create complex queries.

Example 2: Display the surname, DOB and number of points scored for all players aged under 18 who have scored more than 5000 points:

```
SELECT playerSurname, playerDOB, playerPoints
FROM Player
WHERE playerAge < 18
AND playerPoints >= 5000;
```

EXAM TIP

Database queries are carried out using the SQL SELECT statement.

EQUI-JOIN between tables

If a search requires the display of data located in two linked tables, the SELECT clause must specify the link. An EQUI-JOIN is added to the WHERE statement, stating that the primary and foreign key values in both tables must match.

EXAM TIP

An EQUI-JOIN clause can be used in a SELECT statement to allow different tables to be linked.

```
SELECT fieldName1, fieldName2, fieldName3

FROM tableName1, tableName2

WHERE tableName1.fieldName = tableName2.fieldName
AND fieldName = data;
```

Example 3: Display the forename, surname and town of any players who play for a team based in Hamilton:

```
SELECT playerForename, playerSurname, teamTown

FROM Player, Team

WHERE Team.teamID = Player.teamID

AND town. Team = "Hamilton";
```

Example 4: display the forename, surname, number of points scored, team name and team ID for any players who have scored at least 4000 points for a team in the West district. As the teamID field appears in both tables, you must indicate which table you want to use, e.g. player.teamID

```
SELECT playerForename, playerSurname, playerPoints,

teamName, Team.teamID

FROM Team, Player

WHERE (Team.teamID = Player.teamID)

AND (playerPoints >= 4000)

AND (teamDistrict = "West");
```

Sorting

The ORDER BY clause specifies how the output of a search should be sorted. ORDER BY is followed by the name of the field and whether it is ascending (ASC) or descending (DESC) order:

```
SELECT fieldName1, fieldName2, fieldName3

FROM tableName

WHERE fieldName = data

ORDER BY fieldName ascending or descending;
```

Example 5: display the forename, surname, teamID and points scored for any player who has scored fewer than 1000 points this season, with the player who has scored most points listed first:

```
SELECT playerForename, playerSurname, teamID, playerPoints

FROM Player

WHERE playerPoints < 1000

ORDER BY playerPoints DESC;
```

Example 6: display the forename, surname and teamID of all players from teams based in Glasgow. The listing should be in alphabetical order of surname. Players with the same surname should be listed in alphabetical order of first name:

```
SELECT playerForename, playerSurname, Player.TeamID

FROM Player, Team

WHERE teamTown = "Glasgow"

ORDER BY playerSurname ASC, playerForename ASC;
```

Adding records

The INSERT INTO statement is used to add records to a table. The statement is followed by the table name and then the VALUES statement, followed by the data in brackets separated by commas.

```
INSERT INTO tableName (fieldName1, fieldName2) VALUES
(value1, value2);
```

You must ensure that the order of the values is the same as the order of the fields.

Example 7: Details of the latest team to join the league are as follows:

teamID	TEAM007
teamName	Kilbryde Kings
teamDistrict	West
teamTown	East Kilbride
teamVenue	Wright SC
teamContact	John Wilson
teamEmail	KingsEK@gmail.com
teamPhone	01355 263028

You can add a **complete record** to a database, by writing the following SQL statement, using only the values. The values must be present for every field and they must be presented in the same order as the field names in the table.

```
INSERT INTO Team
VALUES ("TEAM007", "Kilbryde Kings", "West", "East Kilbride",
"Wright SC", "John Wilson", "KingsEK@gmail.com",
"01355 263028");
```

If we want to **add partial record data** to a table, both the field names and their associated values must be identified in the SQL statement.

Example 8: A new player has joined the Kilbryde Kings. His details are shown below:

PlayerID	PLAY2048
playerForename	Stewart
playerSurname	Chalmers
teamID	TEAM007

You could add these details to the database using the following SQL:

```
INSERT INTO Player (playerID, playerForename, playerSurname, teamID)
VALUES ("PLAY2048", "Stewart", "Chalmers", "TEAM007");
```

Editing records

The **UPDATE** statement is used to alter records in a table. The statement is followed by the name of the table, a **SET** clause and a **WHERE** clause, which states what criteria must be met.

```
UPDATE tableName
SET fieldName to updated value
WHERE criteria to be met;
```

Example 9: The surname for Player PLAY2048 in the previous example has been misspelt. It should be "Stuart", rather than "Stewart". You could update the correct record of the database by writing the following SQL:

```
UPDATE Player
SET playerForename = "Stuart"
WHERE playerID = "PLAY2048";
```

Example 10: The contact details for the Airdrie Avengers have changed. The team's contact person is now Steve Rogers and the e-mail address is now airdrie@scotsdarts.com.

You could update the database record using the following SQL statement:

```
UPDATE Team
SET teamContact = "Steve Rogers", teamEmail = "airdrie@
scotsdarts.com"
WHERE teamName = "Airdrie Avengers";
```

Deleting records

The **DELETE FROM** statement is used to delete records in a table. The statement is followed by the name of the table and the WHERE clause, which states the criteria to be met.

```
DELETE FROM tableName
     WHERE criteria to be met;
```

Example 11: The Border Reivers have been knocked out of the league. You could remove the correct record from the database by writing the following SQL:

```
DELETE FROM Team
     WHERE teamName = "Border Reivers";
```

Example 12: Jessica Stark has given up darts. You could remove the correct record from the database by writing the following SQL:

```
DELETE FROM Player
     WHERE playerForename = "Jessica"
     AND playerSurname = "Stark";
```

Quick Test 29

1. Which clause is used in an SQL SELECT statement to indicate how the output should be sorted?
2. Which SQL statement is used to add new records to a database?
3. Which SQL statement is used to remove records from a database?
4. Which SQL statement is used to modify existing records in a database?

Testing

Testing of databases is similar to the testing of computer programs described earlier. One of the main aims of testing is to ensure that SQL operations work correctly.

Consider the player table of the Darts League database described earlier:

playerID	player Forename	player Surname	player DOB	player Age	player Points	teamID
PLAY1234	Barry	Soap	10/12/1988	30	9534	TEAM005
PLAY2048	Stuart	Chalmers	19/03/2000	17	6053	TEAM007
PLAY2062	Sue	Richards	27/05/2000	17	7625	TEAM005
PLAY2195	Carole	Danvers	03/10/1978	40	4567	TEAM007
PLAY2248	Jenny	Walters	15/05/1992	28	3082	TEAM005
PLAY2356	John	Wilson	21/06/1993	27	6656	TEAM005
PLAY2447	Jean	Gray	14/08/1986	31	4043	TEAM007
PLAY2559	Anthony	Stark	15/09/1977	47	6842	TEAM005
PLAY2665	Kathleen	Pryde	07/10/1999	19	6092	TEAM007
PLAY2789	Steve	Rogers	04/03/1988	30	4531	TEAM007

A query is required to display the full name and points of all players in TEAM007. The details should be listed in alphabetical order of player surname. The predicted output is as follows:

Forename	Surname	Points
Stuart	Chalmers	6053
Carole	Danvers	4567
Jean	Gray	4043
Kathleen	Pryde	6092
Steve	Rogers	4531

EXAM TIP

All database queries should be tested and evaluated for accuracy of output and fitness for purpose.

Evaluation

We can evaluate queries in terms of accuracy of output and fitness for purpose.

Accuracy of output

If the output is exactly as predicted, with all fields present and sorted correctly we can accept it as accurate. If it is not as predicted, due to missing fields or incorrect sorting, then it is not accurate and the query needs to be checked for errors.

Fitness for purpose

Fitness for purpose measures how well a query is designed and how well it conforms to the design. It considers whether the query does what it's supposed to do, from the point of view of an end user. Some aspects of fitness for purpose are highly visible, for example whether all fields are present and sorted correctly, but other aspects, such as code quality and security, are less visible.

A query may produce accurate output, but take an unacceptably long time to do it, in which case the design of the query, or even the whole database, may need to be reconsidered. Badly-written or malicious queries may introduce errors into the database, by deleting or amending data. If this happens, they are clearly not fit for purpose.

Quick Test 30

1. What is the main aim in testing a database?
2. What must be drawn up before testing a database?
3. What does "accuracy of output" mean in the context of a database?
4. What does "fitness for purpose" mean with respect to a database query?

Data protection

All databases, other than those listed in the exceptions noted below, must meet the requirements of the **Data Protection Act, 1998**. The first Data Protection Act (DPA) became law in 1984, long before rapid growth of the Internet made it easy to share data online.

The Act was revised in 1998 to take account of increased access to online data. The updated Act covered personal data held on paper as well as on computer systems and made it illegal to transfer data to countries that do not have appropriate data protection laws.

The Data Protection Act has two general purposes:

- to define the rights of individuals about which data is held and what they can do regarding data held about them
- to define the responsibilities of data users and processors.

The Act outlines eight principles of good information handling, stating that data must be:

- fairly and lawfully processed
- processed for limited purposes
- adequate, relevant and not excessive
- accurate
- not kept for longer than is necessary
- processed in line with your rights
- secure
- not transferred to other countries without adequate protection.

> **EXAM TIP**
>
> The office of the Data Protection Commissioner oversees the operation of the Data Protection Act.

Three groups are referred to in the Act:

- data subjects
- data users
- data controllers.

Data subjects are the individuals about whom data is held. Under the Act, data subjects have certain rights including:

- knowing if data is held about them on a computer system and being able to get a copy and description of that data
- knowing the purpose(s) for which the data is being processed and who is going to receive the data
- inspecting such data and having it changed if it is incorrect
- seeking compensation if the data held is inaccurate or if unauthorised people have been given access to it
- preventing the processing of data that is likely to cause damage or distress
- ensuring that decisions made against them are not made only by automatic processing.

A data subject is required to pay an administration fee to exercise any of these rights. Once this payment is processed the data subject can apply to the Data Protection Commissioner to prevent the processing of data or to correct or even to delete it.

A **data user** is someone who makes use of personal information for a certain purpose. When carrying out their work, a data user must abide by the DPA, and make sure that the data used is:

- accurate and up-to-date
- relevant and not excessive in relation to the specified purpose
- held and used only for the specified purpose
- used only with the consent of the data subjects and processed in line with their rights
- adequate for the specified purpose
- protected by adequate security, e.g. passwords
- only shared with countries that have appropriate data protection legislation.

A **medical receptionist** could be an example of a data user.

A **data controller** is the person or persons in an organisation placed in charge of the collection and use of personal data.

The Act specifies that the data controller must do the following:

- correctly and accurately complete the registry for the Data Protection Commissioner
- apply to the Data Protection Commissioner for permission to keep the personal data
- specify what data needs to be kept, the purpose it will be used for and who will have access to it.

The DPA allows data subjects to find out the information held about them, whether this is held electronically or on paper.

The **Data Protection Commissioner**, formerly known as the Data Protection Registrar, is the person to contact if a data subject has problems accessing personal data or is concerned about inaccurate information being held. The office of the Data Protection Commissioner oversees the administration of the Act.

One function of the DPA is to ensure that personal data held on data subjects is not held secretly but can be found by the subject. The **Data Protection Register (DPR)** holds the details of which organisations hold information on data subjects. The DPR can be found in public libraries.

There are certain exceptions to the DPA, including:

- national security, e.g. data used to fight terrorism
- crime and taxation, e.g. data used by the Police and other organisations to fight crime
- domestic purposes, e.g. personal data used for family or household reasons.

Quick Test 31

1. Why did the Data Protection Act need to be revised in 1998?
2. What is the meaning of the term "data subjects"?
3. What is the meaning of the term "data controller"?
4. Who is responsible for overseeing the operation of the Data Protection Act?

Analysis

The analysis phase of website design relates mainly to determining the functional requirements of the website, or what it is intended to do. These will depend on what the target users expect the website to do and how they will interact with it. This area is covered in greater detail in the running example below.

Design

Website structure

The design of a website shows the type of **navigational structure** used. This is usually either linear or hierarchical. In a linear design all the pages form a single sequence, for example:

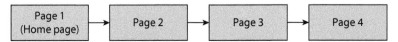

In a hierarchical design, all the pages branch off from a single starting point, for example:

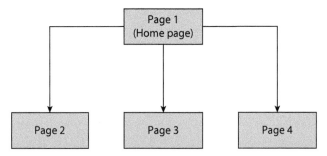

Note that the design shows the direction of each link.

Website example

The Burgh of Coatbank has decided to launch a Music Festival. Four concerts will take place on Friday and Saturday, one each afternoon and one each evening. Each concert will feature a different type of music: Rock, Folk, Classical or Jazz. A new website is being developed to promote the festival. It will consist of five pages, each of which will have a main heading centred at the top of the page. The new website will have a hierarchical structure with the content of the pages as follows:

A home page displaying:
- a brief introduction to the festival
- internal hyperlinks to specialist pages about the four concerts
- an external link to the Coatbank Council website.

Four specialist pages displaying:
- a photo of the band playing at that concert
- a paragraph of information about the band
- a bulleted list of other performers of the featured type of music
- a hyperlink back to the home page.

EXAM TIP

Website designs can be either linear or hierarchical.

The following diagram shows the navigational structure of the Coatbank Music Festival website. The arrows show the direction of the hyperlinks appearing on each page.

```
                          ┌──────────────┐
                          │  Home page   │
                          └──────┬───────┘
        ┌───────────┬───────────┼───────────┬───────────┐
        ▼           ▼           ▼           ▼           ▼
┌──────────────┐┌──────────────┐┌──────────────┐┌──────────────┐┌──────────────┐
│ Rock concert ││ Folk concert ││Classical     ││ Jazz concert ││Coatbank      │
│    page      ││    page      ││concert page  ││    page      ││council home  │
│              ││              ││              ││              ││page          │
└──────────────┘└──────────────┘└──────────────┘└──────────────┘└──────────────┘
```

User interface design

The user-interface design can be illustrated using **wireframes**. A separate wireframe is needed for each page. Each wireframe indicates the intended layout of the page and shows the position of:

- text elements
- media elements (images, audio clips and video clips)
- elements that allow the user to interact with the page
- position and type of all hyperlinks on the page.

The user interface design should take account of end-user requirements, visual layout and readability and should show:

- navigational links
- relative vertical positioning of the media displayed
- file formats of the media (text, graphics, video, and audio).

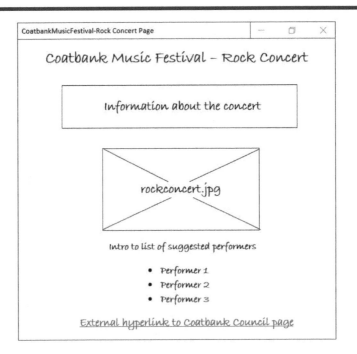

In practice, a similar wireframe would be produced for each of the other Concert pages. The design should be consistent across all the pages.

Quick Test 32

1. At what stage of the design process are the functional requirements of a website determined?

2. In which type of navigational structure do all the pages follow a single sequence?

3. In which type of navigational structure do all the pages branch off from a single starting point?

4. What graphical tool is used extensively in user interface design?

Prototyping

Prototypes are used to show the proposed user interface for a website or any other software product. They are used in usability testing, along with personas (detailed descriptions of typical end users) and test cases. Prototypes can be low-fidelity or high-fidelity. Some developers use both. Low-fidelity prototypes are paper-based, so they can be produced quickly to give potential end users of the software product an idea of the "look and feel" of the product while they interact with it.

High-fidelity prototypes are beyond the scope of this course. They are electronic and are often created using RAD (Rapid Application Development) tools. It doesn't take long to produce a working interface as only the interface is constructed initially. The internal details of processes are ignored, and the screen elements don't actually do anything, other than displaying messages. A high-fidelity prototype allows potential end users to interact with the interface as it will appear in the finished product. This gives users a more realistic idea of how the finished product will look and feel, in comparison to a low-fidelity, paper-based prototype.

During usability testing, potential end users, or testers who adopt an end-user persona, carry out tasks described in test cases using the prototype. Developers will be present to simulate changing of screens, update page content, show the results of a calculation or perform an interaction as the user interacts with the elements of the prototype. Developers can accept user feedback and observe any difficulties that users encounter as they perform the tasks specified in the test cases. This allows them to make amendments to the user interface at a relatively early stage in product development.

Prototypes should be based on the layout indicated in the wireframes. However, unlike wireframes, which are created to ensure consistency and share details with members of the development team, the intended audience of prototypes is end users of the finished product. For this reason, a prototype should show more details for the content and the screen elements that will be used to perform tasks.

Creating low-fidelity prototypes

There are several ways of creating low-fidelity prototypes. For example:

- A simple hand-drawn sketch of the proposed interface is one of the easiest ways of producing a paper-based prototype. Coloured pencils, felt pens and markers can be used to add colour, while drawings of images and other elements can give end users an impression of the interface. Any size of paper can be used but flip-chart paper is easy to handle and encourages collaborative group work.
- Developers can use free prototyping tools, such as the Pencil software produced by Evolus (http://pencil.evolus.vn/). Pencil provides a range of built-in templates for Windows, Android and iOS (Apple). These templates can be used to produce realistic-looking interfaces that can be exported as PNG files and printed as prototypes for usability testing.
- Simple graphics packages such as paint.net (https://www.getpaint.net/) can be used to create the sample layouts using the toolbox provided.

Prototype examples

Simple prototypes, like those shown below, can be created with marker pens and flip-chart paper.

Coatbank Music Festival - Home Page

The first-ever Coatbank Music Festival will take place on Saturday 16 and Sunday 17th June 2018 at the Coatbank Burgh Hall. Concerts will take place each day at 2:00 pm and 7:00 pm. The concerts will cover a range of musical styles including Rock (Saturday afternoon), Folk (Saturday evening), Jazz (Sunday afternoon) and Classical (Sunday evening). Follow the links below for further information.

Saturday Afternoon Rock Concert

Saturday Evening Folk Concert

Sunday Afternoon Jazz Concert

Sunday Evening Classical Concert

Coatbank Council Website

Coatbank Music Festival - Rock Concert

This year's Rock Concert will take place at 2:00 pm on Saturday 16th June. It will feature chart-toppers Little Fix, ably supported by local favourites Coatbank Clique.

Other Rock acts you might like to check out:

- Spicy Girls: one of the earliest Girl Bands
- Deacon Bloo: Scotland's greatest
- Beagles: country-influenced guitar band
- Lead Zeppelin: ultimate heavy rock band

More sophisticated prototypes, such as those shown below, can be created using Pencil templates.

CoatbankMusicFestival - Home Page   _ □ ×

Coatbank Music Festival - Home Page

The first-ever Coatbank Music Festival will take place on Saturday 16th and Sunday 17th June 2018 at the Coatbank Burgh Hall. Concerts will take place each day at 2:00 pm and 7:00 pm. The concerts will cover a range of styles including Rock (Saturday afternoon), Folk (Saturday evening), Jazz (Sunday afternoon) and Classical (Sunday evening). Follow the links below for further information.

Saturday Afternoon Rock Concert
Saturday Evening Folk Concert
Sunday Afternoon Jazz Concert
Sunday Evening Classical Concert
Coatbank Council Website

CoatbankMusicFestival - Rock Concert   _ □ ×

Coatbank Music Festival - Rock Concert

This year's Rock Concert will take place at 2:00 pm on Saturday 16th June. It will feature chart-toppers Little Fix, ably supported by local favourites Coatbank Clique.

Some other Rock acts you might want to check out:

- Spicy Girls one of the earliest Girl Bands
- Deacon Bloo: Scotland's greatest
- Beagles: country-influenced guitar band
- Lead Zeppelin: ultimate heavy rock band

Coatbank Council Website

EXAM TIP

Prototypes showing the user interface for a website are a useful tool for usability testing.

Quick Test 33

1. What are prototypes used for?
2. How are prototypes produced?
3. What are the characteristics of low-fidelity prototypes?
4. What are the characteristics of high-fidelity prototypes?

Implementation

Three distinct languages are widely used in the implementation of websites:

- **HTML** is used to define the **content** of web pages
- **CSS** is used to specify the **layout** of web pages
- **JavaScript** is used to program the **behaviour** of web pages.

We will examine each of these languages in turn.

Implementation (HTML)

Hypertext Markup Language (HTML) is the standard language for creating web pages. It is one of the key technologies of the Web, along with **Cascading Style Sheets (CSS)** and **JavaScript**. Web browsers, such as **Internet Explorer** or **Firefox**, read HTML documents from a local or remote web server and display them as multimedia web pages.

HTML documents are built from **elements** which allow text, images and other objects to be embedded in a web page. They contain headings, paragraphs, lists, links, quotes and other items.

HTML elements are defined by **tags,** written using angle brackets. Tags like <img > and <input > display content directly on a page. Others like <p> ... </p> give further information about document text and can include other tags as sub-elements. Browsers do not display the HTML tags themselves, they use them to determine the content and layout of pages.

HTML documents can embed programs written in scripting languages like **JavaScript** that can affect the behaviour and content of web pages. CSS can be used to define the look and layout of content. The **World Wide Web Consortium (W3C)**, maintains the HTML and CSS standards. The current standard is HTML 5 but older standards are still widely used.

Consider the following simple HTML document:

```
<!DOCTYPE HTML>
<html>
    <head>
        <title>Title of the document</title>
    </head>
    <body>
        Document content ...
    </body>
</html>
```

> **EXAM TIP**
>
> HTML tags define the content and layout of web pages.

Note that the scope of each tag is terminated by the same tag preceded by a slash (/).

!DOCTYPE <!DOCTYPE HTML>

The <!DOCTYPE> declaration should be the first element in any HTML document, before the <html> tag. It is not really an HTML tag. It tells the web browser what version of HTML the page is written in.

You should always place a <!DOCTYPE> declaration at the start of HTML documents, so that the browser knows what type of document to expect.

The following table shows some of the commonest HTML tags.

Tag	Description	Example
<html> tag	Specifies the root of an HTML document.	**<html>** **Content of document** **</html>**
<head> tag	Provides information about the document.	**<head>** **<title>**
<title> tag	Defines a title for the document (mandatory component of <head> element).	**Title of the document** **</title>** **</head>**
<body> tag	Defines the document's body.	**<body>** **Body of document** **</body>**
<header> tag	Defines a header for a document or section.	**<header>** **<h1>Principal heading </h1>** **<h3>Secondary heading </h3>** **<p> Additional information </p>** **</header>**
<p> tag	Defines a paragraph.	
<h1> to <h6> tags	Specify sizes of HTML headings.	
<div> tag	Defines a section in a document. Example defines a section that will be displayed as red text. #FF000 is the hexadecimal colour code for red.	**<div style="color:#FF0000">** **<h3>This is a heading</h3>** **<p>This is a paragraph</p>** **</div>**
<link> tag	Indicates the relationship between a document and an external resource (often used to link to CSS style sheets).	**<head>** **<link rel="stylesheet" type="text/css" href="theme.css">** **</head>**

<a> tag	Anchor tag – defines a hyperlink.	**A link to the SQA website** **<a href="https://www.sqa.org.uk">** **Visit the SQA Website</a>**
<img> tag	Defines an image.	**<img src="smiley.gif" alt="Smiley Face" height="45" width="45">**
<audio> tag	Defines audio content. Text between the <audio> and </audio> tags will be displayed in browsers that do not support the <audio> element.	**<audio controls>** **<source src="song.mp3" type="audio/mpeg">** **Browser does not support audio tag.** **</audio>**
<video tag	Defines video content. Text between the <video> and </video> tags will be displayed in browsers that do not support the <video> element.	**<video width="320" height="240" controls>** **<source src="movie.mp4" type="video/mp4">** **Browser does not support video tag.** **</video>**
<ol> tag	Defines an ordered (numbered) list.	**<ol>** **List items** **</ol>**
<ul> tag	Defines an unordered (bulleted) list.	**<ul>** **List items** **</ul>**
<li> tag	Defines a list item.	**<li> Item 1** **<li> Item 2** **<li> Item 3**

Quick Test 34

1. What are the components of HTML documents?
2. How are HTML elements defined?
3. Which declaration should always be placed at the start of an HTML document?
4. What is the function of HTML hyperlinks?

HTML hyperlinks

Almost every web page has links that allow users to click from page to page or jump to another document. These links are known as hyperlinks. When the mouse is moved over a hyperlink the mouse arrow will turn into a little hand.

Hyperlinks are defined by the <a> tag:

```
<a href="url">link text</a>
```

For example:

```
<a href="https://www.sqa.org.uk/">Visit the SQA website</a>
```

The **href attribute** specifies the destination address (https://www.sqa.org.uk/) and the **link text** is the part displayed to the user (Visit the SQA website).

The **link text** (Visit the SQA website) is the visible part. Clicking here will send you to the address specified.

This example uses a full web address. This is known as an **absolute URL** (Universal Resource Locator). A link within the same website uses a **relative URL**, omitting http:// www.... For example:

```
<a href="html_images.asp">My Images</a>
```

Link colours change depending on their current status:

- unvisited link: underlined and blue
- visited link: underlined and purple
- active link: is underlined and red.

These default colours can be changed using styles:

```
<style>
a:link {
    color: blue;
    background-color: transparent;
    text-decoration: none;
}
a:visited {
    color: green;
    background-color: transparent;
    text-decoration: none;
}
a:active {
    color: yellow;
    background-color: transparent;
    text-decoration: underline;
}
    </style>
```

A **target attribute** can be added to specify where the linked document should be opened. Common values are as follows:

_self: opens in the same window/tab as it was clicked (default)

_blank: opens in a new window or tab

_top: opens the linked document in the full body of the window.

The example below will open the linked document in a new browser window/tab:

```
<a href="https://www.sqa.org.uk/" target="_blank">Visit the
SQA website</a>
```

It is common to use images as links:

```
<a href="default.asp">

    <img src="PythonLogo.gif" alt="Python Tutorial" style="
    width:42px;height:42px;0;">

</a>
```

External pages can either be referenced with a full URL or with a path relative to the current web page. For example:

```
<a href="https://https://www.learnpython.org/default.asp">
Python Tutorial</a>
```

Linking to a page located in the HTML folder on the current website:

```
<a href="/html/default.asp">Python Tutorial</a>
```

Linking to a page located in the same folder as the current page:

```
<a href="default.asp">Python Tutorial</a>
```

The HTML code for the Coatbank Music Festival Home Page might look like this (using the Notepad ++ editor):

This would display as follows in the Internet Explorer browser:

> **Coatbank Music Festival - Home Page**
>
> The first-ever Coatbank Music Festival will take place on Saturday 16th and Sunday 17th June 2018 at the Coatbank Burgh Hall. Concerts will take place each day at 2:00 pm and 7:00 pm. The concerts will cover a range of musical styles including Rock (Saturday afternoon), Folk (Saturday evening), Jazz (Sunday afternoon) and Classical (Sunday evening). Follow the links below for further information.
>
> Saturday Afternoon Rock Concert
> Saturday Evening Folk Concert
> Sunday Afternoon Jazz Concert
> Saturday Evening Classical Concert
> Coatbank Council Website

Quick Test 35

1. What is the anchor tag <a> used for in HTML?
2. What tag is used to define a numbered list in HTML?
3. Which HTML tag indicates the relationship between a document and an external resource?
4. How can the default colour scheme for hyperlinks be changed?

Implementation (CSS)

CSS (Cascading Style Sheets) describes how HTML elements should be displayed. It can control the layout of multiple web pages.

HTML was originally created to describe the content of a web page. It wasn't meant to contain tags like <font>, and colour attributes for formatting pages. When these tags were added, development of large websites, where fonts and colour information might be needed on every single page, became difficult and expensive.

The World Wide Web Consortium (W3C) developed CSS to remove style formatting from HTML documents.

CSS Syntax and selectors

A CSS rule-set consists of a Selector and a Declaration Block:

Selector	Declaration		Declaration
h1	{color:green;		font-size:10px;}
	Property Value		Property Value

The **Selector** points to the HTML element to be styled. The **Declaration Block** contains one or more declarations, separated by semicolons. Each declaration includes a CSS **property name**, followed by a colon and a value. A CSS declaration always ends with a semicolon. Declaration blocks are inside curly brackets. In the following example all <p> elements will be left-aligned, with a green text colour:

```
p {
    color: green;
    text-align: left;
}
```

There are three ways of inserting a style sheet: external, internal or inline.

An **external style sheet** lets you change the appearance of an entire website by changing a single file. Each page should include a reference to the external style sheet file, inside the <link> element, within the <head> section. For example:

```
<head>
    <link rel="stylesheet" type="text/css" href="style1.css">
</head>
```

An **external style sheet** should not contain any HTML tags. It can be written using any text editor and must be saved with a .css extension. Here's what "style1.css" looks like:

```
body {
    background-color: lightblue;
}
h1 {
    color: navy;
    margin-left: 12px;
}
```

An internal style sheet can be useful if a single page has a unique style. It should be inside the <style> element, within the <head> section of the HTML page:

```
<head>
    <style>
        body {
            background-color: yellow;
        }
        h1 {
             color: blue;
             margin-left: 30px;
        }
    </style>
</head>
```

An **inline style** can be used to apply a unique style to a single element by adding a style attribute, containing any CSS property, to the relevant element. For example, to change the colour and the left margin of an <h1> element:

```
<h1 style="color:black;margin-left:20px;">
This is a heading</h1>
```

Inline styles should be used sparingly since, by mixing content with presentation, they lose many of the advantages of a style sheet.

Quick Test 36

1. Why was CSS (Cascading Style Sheets) developed?
2. What does a CSS rule set consist of?
3. What is an internal style sheet used for?
4. What would you use to style a single element in CSS?

CSS Selectors

EXAM TIP

A CSS rule set consists of a Selector and a Declaration Block.

CSS selectors can be used to locate or select HTML elements based on element name, id, class, attribute and other features.

The **element selector** selects elements based on the element name. For example, you could select all <p> elements on a page as follows:

```
p {
    text-align: left;
    color: darkblue;
}
```

In this example, all <p> elements will be left-aligned, with a dark blue text colour.

The **id selector** uses the id attribute of an HTML element to select a specific element. The id of an element should be unique within a page. You can select an element with a specific id by writing a hash character (#), followed by the id of the element, for example, the following style rule would be applied to the HTML element with id = "first":

```
#first {
    text-align: left;
    color: darkblue;
}
```

The **class selector** selects elements with a specific class attribute. To select elements with a specific class, write a period (.) character, followed by the name of the class. In the following example, all HTML elements with class="left" will be dark blue and left-aligned:

```
.left {
    text-align: left;
    color: darkblue;
}
```

You can also specify that only specific HTML elements should be affected by a class. In the following example, only <p> elements with class="right" will be right-aligned and green:

```
p.right {
    text-align: right;
    color: green;
}
```

HTML elements can refer to more than one class. In the following example, the <p> element will be styled according to class="left" and to class="large":

```
<p class="left large">This paragraph refers to two classes.</p>
```

Elements with the same style definitions can be grouped together. Consider the following example:

```
h1 {
    text-align: left;
    color: black;
}
h2 {
    text-align: left;
    color: black;
}
p {
    text-align: left;
    color: black;
}
```

This could be improved by grouping the selectors together, separated by commas:

```
h1, h2, p {
    text-align: left;
    color: black;
}
```

You should be able to read and explain code that makes use of CSS. Careful study of the above examples will help you to do this.

Quick Test 37

1. What would be the effect of the following CSS element selector?
    ```
    p {
        text-align: right;
        color: darkblue;
    }
    ```
2. What would be the effect of the following CSS class selector?
    ```
    .left {
        text-align: left;
        color: darkblue;
    }
    ```
3. What would be the effect of the following CSS class selector?
    ```
    p.right {
        text-align: right;
        color: green;
    }
    ```
4. What would be the effect of the following CSS style definition?
    ```
    h1, h2, p {
        text-align: left;
        color: black;
    }
    ```

Implementation (JavaScript)

JavaScript is a programming language used to carry out complex tasks on websites. If a web page does more than displaying static information, for example, displaying content updates, interactive maps or animated graphics, JavaScript is probably involved. One important feature of JavaScript is the handling of events. JavaScript **event handlers** are JavaScript code added inside the HTML tags, that execute JavaScript when something happens, such as pressing a button or moving your mouse over a link, submitting a form etc. Their basic syntax is as follows:

```
name_of_handler="JavaScript code here"
```

For example:

```
<a href="http://google.com" onClick="alert('hello!')">Google</a>
```

This is inside a HTML tag, via the **onClick** event handler. When the link is clicked, the user will see an alert message before being taken to Google. Different event handlers work with different HTML tags. For example, while "onClick" can be inserted into most HTML tags, other event handlers like "onLoad" can only be used inside the <body> and <img> tags. Below are some of the main event handlers supported by JavaScript.

Event handler	Purpose
onClick	Used to invoke JavaScript upon clicking (a link, or form boxes)
onLoad	Used to invoke JavaScript after the page or an image has finished loading
onMouseOver	Used to invoke JavaScript if the mouse passes by some link
onMouseOut	Used to invoke JavaScript if the mouse goes past some link
onUnload	Used to invoke JavaScript right after someone leaves this page

We can use **onMouseOver** and **onMouseOut** to help us detect where the mouse pointer is on the screen with reference to a particular page element, such as a graphic or a text box. The onMouseOver event is fired when the mouse cursor enters the region of the screen occupied by the relevant element. The onMouseOut event occurs when the cursor leaves that same region.

The following example shows the use of JavaScript code within HTML. When the mouse is moved into the text box a red border will appear. When it is moved back out the border will vanish.

Move the mouse pointer into and out of this text box

```
<head>
    <script type="text/javascript">
        function OnMouseOver (textbox) {
            textbox.style.border = "2px solid red";
        }
        function OnMouseOut (textbox) {
            textbox.style.border = "";
        }
    </script>
</head>
<body>
    <div style="background-color:#d0f0a0; width:200px"
        onmouseover="OnMouseOver (this)" onmouseout="OnMouseOut
        (this)">
        Move the mouse pointer into and out of this text box
    </div>
</body>
```

Quick Test 38

1. What new functionality does JavaScript add to web pages?
2. Where is JavaScript code normally inserted?
3. What feature allows JavaScript to be executed when something happens?
4. What does JavaScript use to detect where the mouse pointer is on the screen with reference to a page element, such as a graphic or a text box?

GOT IT? ☐ ☐ ☐

Testing

Testing

Testing websites is similar to testing computer programs. When testing a website we need to ensure that:

- implementation matches the user-interface design
- all links and other navigational elements work correctly
- all media elements (such as text, graphics, and video) display correctly
- everything works consistently throughout the webside.

User interface

Before a user interface (UI) is created it has to first be designed. This usually involves a drawing or a graphic of what the user should see when using the system. It is important that the UI matches this design. All the screens that a user will come across in the system must been designed in this way. The design will show what each element of the UI should do, and these elements will be tested.

Here is a list of some tests that can be performed.

- Check the layout matches the design.
- Check that the spelling is correct.
- Check that scroll functions, audio, and video clips run without problems.
- Check that the buttons of the page work.
- Check the texts, fonts, colours and sizes match the original design.

Navigation

Navigation testing is carried out on an information system to ensure that when a user is working with it they can navigate through the software as intended. All links are tested to ensure that they link to the appropriate part of the system, and that all page transitions work correctly.

Here is a list of some navigation tests that can be performed.

- Check there are no broken links or hyperlinks.
- Check for smooth transitions between screens.
- Check all hyperlinks work correctly.
- Check all links within the application work.

EXAM TIP

Have a look at an information system and write-up what testing you think would have been done for that specific system.

Quick Test 39

1. Why do we need to test an information system?
2. What does navigation testing do?
3. What are two tests that can be carried out under navigation testing?
4. What should the design of a user interface show?
5. Name two tests carried out to check if the user interface matches the design.

Media elements 1

Consistency

Four types of consistency should be considered when designing websites.

Visual consistency	Page elements like fonts, sizes, buttons and labelling need to be used consistently across the website.
Functional consistency	Similar controls should operate in the same way. For example, going back to a previous page should be done in the same way across the site. This helps increase user confidence in their ability to use the site.
Internal consistency	This is a combination of visual and functional consistency across the site. It improves usability. If new features are introduced, users will find them easier to use if internal consistency is maintained.
External consistency	Design should be consistent across multiple systems/products. This means that the user's experience of one product can be applied to another product in the same suite. For example, all of the Microsoft Office products (Word, Excel, PowerPoint etc.) have a similar user interface.

Evaluation

We can evaluate websites for fitness for purpose.

Fitness for purpose

Fitness for purpose measures how well a website is designed and how well it conforms to the design. It considers whether the site does what it's supposed to do, from the point of view of an end user. Some aspects of fitness for purpose are highly visible, for example whether all elements are present and located correctly, but other aspects like code quality and security are less visible.

A website may behave correctly but take an unacceptably long time to do so. The design may need to be reconsidered. Badly-written websites that allow hackers access are not fit for purpose.

File formats

File storage

There are many different ways to store files, but choosing the correct one can reduce the amount of backing storage needed. Some file types compress data, which allows the file to be transferred faster over a network. We experience this benefit when downloading files from the Internet. The smaller the file, the faster it will download.

There are two compression techniques you need to know about: **lossy** and **lossless**.

Compression techniques
- **Lossy:** when a file is compressed using this technique, **data is lost** during the process. Sometimes the loss of data is not noticeable, but the more a file is compressed using this technique the more noticeable the loss of data becomes.
- **Lossless:** when a file is compressed using a lossless technique, **no data is lost** during the process. Lossless compression is used in cases where it is important that the original and the decompressed data are identical, such as executable programs or text files.

File types

Text
- **txt:** this is a standard text document that contains **unformatted text** – it is recognised by any word processing and text editing software packages. Various hardware devices, such as smartphones and E-readers, recognise plain text files.
- **RTF (rich text format):** is a common text file format. It supports **several types of text formatting**, such as bold, italics, different fonts and font sizes. RTFs can also save images that are included in the text file.

Audio

- **WAV (waveform audio file format):** this is a digital audio file format used for storing waveform data. It is usually uncompressed, but can use lossless compression. Audio can be saved with **different sampling rates** and **different bit rates**, usually 44.1 KHz, 16 bit, and stereo format (CD quality).

- **MP3:** a compressed audio format that produces near CD quality sound in a file roughly 10% the size of a WAV file. The MP3 format is very popular because of the high-quality to low-file-size ratio. It uses lossy compression, where audio that the human ear cannot detect is removed first. This reduces the file size significantly, but not the quality.

Quick Test 40

1. Name a sound file format that uses lossy compression.
2. Why do some files need to be compressed?
3. What compression technique does not lose data during the process?
4. What type of compression does MP3 use?
5. What text file is capable of storing text formatting?

Media elements 2

Graphics

EXAM TIP

JPEGs are used to store digital images as they can store over 16 million colours.

- **JPEG (Joint Photographic Experts Group):** is a graphic format that can support up to **24-bit** colour (true colour). JPEGs are good for storing digital images. JPEGs use lossy compression. The level of compression can be adjusted.

- **BMP (bitmap):** a bitmap is made up of a grid of pixels. The pixels of a black and white image are stored as 1s and 0s. Each pixel is 1 bit in size. Colour bitmap images can be very large in size, as each pixel can contain different colour depths. The higher the colour depth, the more colours that pixels can represent. Bitmaps are uncompressed, and may require a lot of backing storage.

- **GIF (graphics interchange format):**
GIF is based on an **8-bit** colour code meaning that it is capable of representing a maximum of 256 colours. Because of this limitation, GIFs are used mainly for charts, cartoons, navigation buttons in websites etc. GIF uses a **lossless** compression technique, and can support transparency so that part of an image can blend into the background. GIFs can also be animated (animated gif).

- **PNG (portable network graphic):**
contains a bitmap of indexed colours and uses **lossless** compression, similar to a GIF file commonly used to store graphics for web images. While GIF images only support fully opaque or fully transparent pixels, PNG images allow the image colours to fade from opaque to transparent.

EXAM TIP

Remember which media types use lossless, and which use lossy compression.

Video

- **MPEG (Moving Picture Experts Group):** MPEG files are popular video files. They are compressed by cutting out any unchanged data from frames in the video (lossy compression). When an MPEG video is played back, it is uncompressed, meaning the viewer does not notice the difference.
- **AVI (Audio Video Interleave):** AVI is what is known as a multimedia container file. It stores the video and audio data in a single file, and is not compressed. This limits the quality of the video and audio that can be stored.

PDF (Portable Document Format) files

PDFs were created by Adobe and work on multiple platforms. They are used for attachments in e-mails, or for saving documents in a standard format for viewing on different computer systems. They can **contain text**, **images**, **graphs** etc. and appear exactly the same on screen as they will when printed. Google and other search engines now index PDF documents, allowing users to search for them online. They can be viewed online using Adobe Reader plug-in.

Quick Test 41

1. What video file type uses lossy compression?
2. How many bits can JPEG images support?
3. What are the pixels of a black and white bitmap stored as?
4. Name three standard file formats for graphics.

Factors affecting file size and quality

The storage size and the quality of a file depend on a number of factors. Graphics files will be affected by the **resolution** of the image and the **colour depth** of the image. Sound files will be affected by the **sampling rate** of the sound as well as the **sample depth**. The larger the files you have in your information system, the more storage space you will need. A website that has lots of high-quality images will also take more time to download.

Resolution

Resolution is the measure of the size of the pixels in an image. High-resolution graphics have a large number of small pixels. Low-resolution images have a small number of large pixels. A high-resolution graphic is of a better quality, but requires more storage space. Resolution is usually measured in dots per inch (DPI).

Colour depth

The colour depth is the number of bits used to store the colour of each pixel. The higher the colour depth, the more colours can be represented, thus improving the quality of an image.

EXAM TIP

Digital cameras store photographs using 24-bit colour depth. This is called True Colour.

Image type	Bit depth	Colours	File size for an image 3" × 3" at a resolution of 600 dpi
Black and white	1 bit	2 colours	395.5 KB
GIF	8 bit	256 colours	3.08 MB
JPEG	24 bit	16.7 million colours	9.26 MB

A high colour depth graphic is of a better quality, but requires more storage space.

Sampling rate

This is the number of samples per second in a sound file. The higher the sampling rate, the better the quality of sound, as there are more samples of the sound taken per second. A common sample rate of CD quality sound is 44.1KHz. That is 44,100 samples per second.

Compression

Compression is needed with graphic and sound files to reduce the storage size required. However, by compressing a file, we also reduce the quality of that file. There is a trade-off between quality and file size.

When designing an information system it is important not to have files that are taking up too much space, but equally if the system is, for example, a website selling something, then the pictures need to be of good quality. There are two types of compression you need to know about: **lossy** and **lossless**.

Lossy compression

This type of compression removes some of the data in a file and only keeps what is deemed necessary. In a graphic for example, colours and shades that humans cannot differentiate between are removed first. If we kept on compressing the file, there would be a noticeable reduction in quality as more colours and shades are removed. MPEG, JPEG and MP3 all use lossy compression.

Lossless compression

No data is lost when a file is compressed. It does this by using a code to store patterns of bits that occur repeatedly throughout the file. GIF uses this type of compression.

EXAM TIP

Know which type of compression is used with different files.

Quick Test 42

1. How many colours can a GIF store?
2. What is resolution, and what is it measured in?
3. What is the bit depth used in a JPEG?
4. What is sampling rate?
5. Why do we need to compress graphic and sound files?

Copyright, Designs and Patents Act

When creating websites, it is essential that you use only content that you have created yourself or have licenced from the copyright owner. Failure to do so can incur severe penalties. Content providers, such as stock image suppliers, are extremely vigilant in checking for unauthorised use of their content.

The **Copyright, Designs and Patents Act, 1988** aims to protect all types of Intellectual Property (IP) by ensuring that the authors or creators of a work can receive both credit and compensation. The Act covers all types of IP including written works, television and films but we shall concentrate on the aspects that relate to computing.

Copyright does not need to be registered or recorded. It comes into effect immediately a new work is created. However, it may be to the advantage of copyright holders to register their copyright in case they need to prove ownership at some later date. The UK Copyright Service provides registration for various creators including writers, musicians, artists, designers and software vendors.

Designs are the appearance or construction of a device or other artefact. For example, an iPad has a distinctive design that has been widely imitated. However, the complete design has not been copied as doing so would infringe Apple's registered design. Designs are not automatically protected. They must be registered with the appropriate office.

A **patent** grants exclusive rights to an individual or company for a particular design or process, for a specified time period, in exchange for the public disclosure of the design. Patents must be registered with the patent office and must be original.

Some companies have attempted to patent software and programming techniques. There are fears that, if this trend continues, innovation in software design will slow down and new software products will require patent payments to numerous companies, effectively stifling their creation.

Copyright law plays a significant role in relation to **file sharing networks**. Such networks are not in themselves illegal but using them to distribute copyrighted music and video for free is prohibited. Music industry organisations, such as the Recording Industry Association of America (RIAA) have prosecuted major uploaders of shared files and have attempted prosecution of individual users who have downloaded files.

The Electronic Frontier Foundation (EFF) believe that RIAA has been a bit heavy handed, and support an approach that permits file sharing, but allows copyright holders to receive payment.

Other organisations, including the Federation Against Software Theft (FAST) and the Business Software Alliance (BSA), investigate software piracy and prosecute offenders. Copyright infringement can lead to:

> **EXAM TIP**
> Copyright does not need to be registered. It comes into force automatically when an artefact is created.

- orders to pay damages
- orders restraining copying, displaying or broadcasting of the work
- orders to hand over profits
- orders to hand over all copies.

In serious cases of copyright infringement, courts have been known to grant copyright owners search warrants to track down the sources for bootleg operations. Severe infringement can lead to criminal penalties, including imprisonment, fines and confiscation of copyright material and the equipment used to produce it. These are intended to catch copying on an industrial scale for commercial gain, particularly piracy or counterfeiting of videos and computer software.

Quick Test 43

1. What is the main Act of Parliament that protects Intellectual Property?
2. Does copyright need to be registered or recorded?
3. What is the difference between a design and a patent?
4. Is the use of file sharing networks always illegal?

Quick test answers

Quick Test 1

1. Some stages may need to be repeated due to problems encountered at a later stage.
2. The Waterfall Model.
3. The Evaluation stage.

Quick Test 2

1. The main purpose of the Analysis stage is to identify the functional requirements of the software.
2. A Computer System.
3. Inputs.
4. Work carried out on the input data.
5. Outputs.

Quick Test 3

1. A PDL does not have the same strict syntax as a programming language.
2. A decision.
3. A rectangle with a stripe at each side.
4. Pseudocode or Program Design Language (PDL).

Quick Test 4

1. Wireframing.
2. A flowchart.
3. A loop
4. Pseudocode.

Quick Test 5

1. A linear group of data items of the same type.
2. No.
3. Floating point or Real.
4. A String.

Quick Test 6

1. The print function.
2. It is a comment.
3. Console.
4. The int () function.
5. The float () function.

Quick Test 7

1. 5.75
2. 1024
3. –1
4. 7.0
5. 4.0

Quick Test 8

1. Sequence.
2. Iteration.
3. Selection.
4. For loop.
5. print(round (Result, 4)).

Quick Test 9

1. The if statement.
2. The elif clause.
3. Python uses nested if statements to handle multiple conditions.
4. The operators are == (equality) and != (inequality).
5. Comparison operators can be combined using **and** and **or**.

Quick Test 10

1. For loop.
2. While loop.
3. For loop.
4. (1, 11)
5. False.

Quick Test 11

1. The sum() function.
2. String.
3. The math module.
4. Pi and e.

Quick Test 12

1. Input validation.
2. Searching.
3. Sorting.
4. Traversal.

Quick Test 13

1. Syntax error.
2. Run-time error.
3. Logic error.
4. During compilation or interpretation.
5. If the program appears to run successfully but the output is incorrect.

Quick Test 14

1. Exceptional data.
2. Extreme data.
3. Exceptional data.
4. Extreme data.

Quick Test 15

1. "Fitness for purpose" refers to how well software is designed and how well it conforms to the design.
2. "Robustness" means ensuring that a program will deal correctly with any data input, whether or not the data is correct.
3. Loops.
4. 1-dimensional array.

Quick Test 16

1. 0 to 65,535.
2. The mantissa.
3. One of the bits is used to represent the sign.
4. Each character is assigned a numeric code.

Quick Test 17

1. The range of numbers that can be represented.
2. Scientific notation, scientific form or standard form.
3. 256
4. .0678

Quick Test 18

1. 179
2. 218
3. 01111011
4. 11111101

Quick Test 19

1. 8 bits.
2. Unicode.
3. Bitmapped image.
4. Vector image.

Quick Test 20

1. The data bus.
2. The control bus.
3. Connecting a monitor.
4. A USB interface.

Quick Test 21

1. Reduced instruction set computer (RISC).
2. Lexical analysis.
3. False. Compilers and Interpreters can exist for the same language.
4. Optimisation.

Quick Test 22

1. The interpreter never has access to the whole program – it processes the program line by line.
2. Intermediate code or Bytecode.
3. A computer program that emulates a real machine.
4. If changes are made to the program they can be tested immediately without having to wait for the program to be recompiled.

Quick Test 23

1. Ambient light sensor.
2. To save energy.
3. A firewall.
4. Encryption.

Quick Test 24

1. Flat file database.
2. Relational database.
3. Addition, deletion and amendment.
4. Determining the functional requirements of the database.

Quick Test 25

1. They are used to establish relationships between entities.
2. Primary (main) keys and foreign keys.
3. A one-to-many relationship.
4. Crow's feet notation.

Quick Test 26

1. It provides additional information about the attributes of each table.
2. The entity name and the primary and foreign keys.
3. Attribute name, attribute type, size or precision and validation rules (if required).
4. Validation.

Quick Test 27

1. Tables, fields, search criteria and sort order (where relevant).
2. Referential integrity ensures that the relationships between tables remain accurate by preventing the entry of inaccurate data or linking to data that doesn't exist.
3. Create tables, define relationships, add data.
4. By linking a primary key to foreign keys.

Quick Test 28

1. The general format is:

   SELECT *fields*
   FROM *tables*
   WHERE *conditions*

2. By using the relational operators: AND, OR, <, >, =
3. A maximum of two.

Quick Test 29

1. ORDER BY
2. INSERT INTO
3. DELETE FROM
4. UPDATE

Quick Test 30

1. Ensuring that SQL operations work correctly.
2. Details of the predicted output.
3. The output is exactly as predicted, with all fields present and sorted correctly.
4. Fitness for purpose measures how well a query is designed and how well it conforms to the design.

Quick Test 31

1. To take account of increased online access to data.
2. Data subjects are the individuals about whom data is held.
3. A data controller is the person or persons in an organisation placed in charge of the collection and use of personal data.
4. The Data Protection Commissioner.

Quick Test 32

1. The design stage.
2. A linear structure.
3. A hierarchical structure.
4. Wireframes.

Quick Test 33

1. Prototypes are used to show the proposed user interface for a website or software product.
2. They can be hand-drawn, or they can be produced using graphics software or specialised prototyping tools.
3. Low-fidelity prototypes are paper-based and can be produced quickly to give potential end users of a software product an idea of its "look and feel".
4. High-fidelity prototypes are electronic and are often created using RAD (Rapid Application Development) tools.

Quick Test 34

1. HTML documents are built from elements which allow text, images and other objects to be embedded in a web page.
2. HTML elements are defined by tags, written using angle brackets.
3. A <!DOCTYPE> declaration should be placed at the start of HTML documents, so that the browser knows what type of document to expect.
4. Hyperlinks allow users to click from page to page or jump to another document.

Quick Test 35

1. The anchor tag <a> is used to define a hyperlink.
2. The <ol> tag is used to define a numbered (ordered) list.
3. The <link> tag indicates the relationship between a document and an external resource.
4. The default colours for hyperlinks can be changed by using styles.

Quick Test 36

1. CSS was developed to remove style formatting from HTML documents.
2. A CSS rule set consists of a selector and a declaration block.
3. An internal style sheet is used to style a single page.
4. An inline style would be used to style a single element.

Quick Test 37

1. All <p> elements will be right-aligned, with a dark blue text colour.
2. All HTML elements with class="left" will be dark blue and left-aligned.
3. Only <p> elements with class="right" will be right-aligned and green.
4. All <h1>, <h2> and <p> elements will be left-aligned and black.

Quick Test 38

1. It allows the display of dynamic information such as interactive maps or animated graphics.
2. JavaScript code is normally inserted inside HTML tags.
3. Event handlers allow JavaScript to be executed when something happens.
4. The onMouseOver and onMouseOut event handlers are used to detect where the mouse pointer is on the screen.

Quick Test 39

1. To make sure that it is working for the purpose it was intended for.
2. Navigation ensures that the user can navigate around a system.
3. Any two: check there are no broken links or hyperlinks; check for smooth transitions between screens; check all hyperlinks work correctly; check all links within the application work.
4. What each element of the user interface should do.
5. Any two: check the layout matches the design; check that the spelling is correct; check scroll functions, audio and video clips run without problems; check that the buttons of the page work; check the texts, fonts, colours and sizes match the original design.

Quick Test 40

1. MP3.
2. To transfer over a network faster and to reduce the file size.
3. Lossless.
4. Lossy.
5. RTF.

Quick Test 41

1. MPEG.
2. 24 bit.
3. 1 or 0.
4. BMP, JPEG, GIF.

Quick Test 42

1. 256.
2. Amount of pixels in an image. DPI.
3. 24 bit.
4. The number of samples per second in a sound file.
5. The files are very large in size, and take up lots of storage.

Quick Test 43

1. The Copyright, Designs and Patents Act, 1988.
2. No, it automatically comes into effect when an artefact is created.
3. Designs are the appearance or construction of a device or other artefact. Patents grant exclusive rights for a design or process, for a specified period.
4. No, but it is illegal to use them to distribute copyrighted material.